pint size

To John

Have a great Christmas

Thanks a lot for the help this year

enjoy the Book

all the Best

P.S. all the Best for the year 2001

Keep the good work up with the 2nd team

Pint size

Andy Gregory: Heroes and Hangovers

Phil Thomas & Andy Gregory

EDINBURGH AND LONDON

First published in Great Britain in 2000 by
MAINSTREAM PUBLISHING COMPANY (EDINBURGH) LTD
7 Albany Street
Edinburgh EH1 3UG

ISBN 1 84018 292 X

A catalogue record for this book is available from the British Library

Typeset in Sabon and Univers
Printed and bound in Great Britain by Creative Print and Design Wales

TO LAUREN

3 MARCH 1987 –
THE BEST DAY OF MY LIFE

DAD

Contents

FOREWORD

by Ian Rush

Andy Gregory has, for me, not only been the best rugby league player in the world but also one of the most genuine blokes you could ever wish to meet. A lot of people will tell you one thing and be thinking another – but not Andy. He certainly doesn't hide his feelings and, whether he thinks it's right or wrong, he will give it to you straight.

I remember when he was coach at Salford, he did superbly well in his first couple of seasons in charge. But when it got a little tougher for him he didn't try to hide away and let others take the blame; he remained up front and brutally honest, to the point where it probably offended a few people at times. But that is just the way he is: he isn't scared to call a spade a shovel, and I say more power to his elbow because of it.

I've known him for a good few years now, after we first met through a mutual friend called Phil Lynch. He came to a few Liverpool games during my time at Anfield, and I always thought he was a dyed-in-the-wool Liverpudlian – until it suddenly dawned on me that he only ever seemed to come when we played Manchester United. But even though he does support United, we get on very well. Andy likes good football, the same as he likes good rugby league, and I know there are a lot of people within our sport who have a lot of time for him.

I have spoken to a few of the United lads, like Mark Hughes, who have told me that Andy used to go and watch all their European games, home and away. There was one particular match in Turkey, probably when they were playing Galatasaray, and the security was ridiculously tight. No one could move an inch without someone asking for a pass, or demanding to know why you wanted to go there – when all of a sudden Andy pops up on the pitch itself! That was typical of him: he'd get himself in anywhere, and the fact that he manages to get away with it is another sign of the respect that people have for the man.

Another time, after I had moved to Newcastle, he drove Phil up there to the hotel where I was staying. After a while I had to leave to go to the match, but Andy hung about and took my wife, Tracy, and my two boys to the game, when there was no reason for him to have stayed around. It was only a little thing but it meant a lot to me, and as far as I am concerned, if I can do anything to help him I will. That's why I was more than happy to help him out when he opened a pub, by going along for a few drinks with him on his first night. I remember more recently when he had his radio show in Spain, and he phoned me and Steve McManaman to ask us to take part. If it had just been an ordinary show we would probably not have bothered, but because it was Andy we were more than happy to do interviews with him.

He is respected throughout the entire sporting world, and has put himself out for so many people in his life that it is the least I can do to put myself out a little for him in return by writing this foreword. Maybe it's because he is such a nice guy that some people have taken advantage of him in the past – because I think Andy genuinely believes that everyone is like him. He was the top of the tree as a rugby player, and he remains top of the tree as a person. I hope he gets the rich rewards he deserves.

Ian Rush
Liverpool and Wales

FOREWORD

by Neil Fairbrother

I first got to know Andy when he signed for Warrington, about 13 years ago, and within about ten minutes of meeting him I felt like he had been around for a lifetime. And I mean that in the nicest possible sense as well, Greg!

He came to live in Grappenhall village, where I grew up, and moved into a house about 20 yards from my parents. I had actually just moved out of the area, but I saw a lot of him whenever I visited my folks and we became good friends.

Andy used to wander around the village a lot, and by the time I met him he knew just about everyone. That sums him up for me: a real sporting superstar in his chosen field, but a down to earth guy who always has time for everyone, from the youngest fan who is looking for an autograph or a picture, to the old guy who wants to talk rugby.

As a Warrington fan, I thought it was fantastic. Not only was he doing the business on the field for my team, he was a neighbour and a mate as well. It was great to have a drink and a joke with someone who was a hero to so many people, but who remained a normal guy who would mix with anyone who wanted to talk to him. And there were plenty who did, believe me.

I still remember reading the news that he had signed for Wigan in 1987. At the time I had thought that Warrington were going to build a team around him, and that we were destined for great things. Without Andy, it was pretty clear that we would struggle to win as much as maybe we would have hoped. From my own purely personal and biased point of view, it was a terrible move. From Andy's point – and I wished him all the best as a person – obviously it was a step in the right direction. I know that all the success Wigan subsequently enjoyed wasn't down only to him, but as the scrum-half and pivotal member of the team, he probably played a bigger part than anyone else. Don't forget, at that stage Wigan could buy just about any player they wanted, so for him to be the main cog in such a powerful machine speaks volumes. There can be no doubts that he was the best scrum-half in the world back then.

Like a lot of sportsmen, Andy didn't just restrict himself to his own game, and when he lived in Grappenhall he played quite a few cricket matches for the village third team. It wasn't that he couldn't have coped with a higher standard, but wasn't available to play every week, and it was more of a relaxing, social thing for him. The lads used to love him playing their side – although I have to admit that I personally have never managed to see him play!

He has been in the changing-room at Lancashire quite a few times, and he knows the lads there pretty well. It says a lot that they all to a man enjoy his company, and I know that for his part Andy loves his cricket as well. When I was asked to contribute to his book, I must say I didn't give it a moment's hesitation.

Andy Gregory has done so much for so many over the years, both in terms of entertaining the fans and the countless hours when he has put himself out for others, that it is an absolute pleasure. Best of luck, Andy – I'm proud and privileged to call you a friend.

Neil Fairbrother
Lancashire and England

ONE

The Pie-Eyed Pie Eater

The retching had stopped a couple of hours earlier, about the same time that the walls finally slowed down and the light came back into focus. But the terrible feeling of slipping deeper and deeper into a bottomless pit and the dreadful aching in my stomach just wouldn't go away.

I think that was the night when it really hit me for the first time. Here was Andy Gregory, professional rugby league player, winner of the lot with Wigan and Great Britain, one of the most famous men ever to play the game, lying in bed drunk again, in an unfurnished flat above a run-of-the-mill boozer in Newton-le-Willows.

It should have been one of the most memorable nights of my sporting life outside of rugby league, after my beloved Manchester United had given Juventus a European Cup hiding at Old Trafford. Instead, I couldn't even remember watching the game, after spending another full day in the pub knocking back God knows how many pints of Guinness with anyone who'd talk to me. Just another normal day at the office, really, for yours truly. Only this time the difference was, I realised it.

It had taken one broken marriage, a daughter who didn't want anything to do with me, and a career that had gone to the brink of oblivion to reach that stage – but reach it I most definitely had. Although I guess that there will be some wise guys who would say that, once you had stooped as low as me, there was only one way left to go.

I have always liked a drink, from the days when Geoff Dodge, Ste Clare and I used to skip theory classes in Bolton to spend the afternoon on the pop. After a morning cooking at Greater Universal Stores, where we were studying to become chefs, we would head down town to get pissed. Many's the time the ticket collector woke me from a drunken slumber in Southport, and I had to get a return train back home to Ince.

The problem was that while the others grew up, married and got a completely new set of priorities, mine remained the same: drink, drink and more drink. And while my mates used to save up and look forward to the weekend, I was catapulted into the limelight as a teenager, going from £48 a week at GUS one minute, to a Widnes Wembley hero with a pocketful of beer tokens the next.

To be honest, I should have noticed the warning signs four days after my first ever trip to Wembley, in 1981. A Thursday spent celebrating with my team-mates came to an abrupt end when I was asked to blow into the bag, and I kissed goodbye to my licence for 18 months. Since then there had been another booze-induced driving ban, the threat of a jail sentence and an oceanful of drink. True, there has been the odd laugh along the way, but there has also been a hell of a lot of soul-searching.

As recently as 1999 I would get up, take training at Salford and be in the pub by 11. The dinner time crew would come in, and Andy Greg would be there to keep them company. Then the tea-time shift would replace them, and yours truly would again be a willing accomplice. Eight o'clock would arrive, along with the lads out for the night, and there would be another day gone. Welcome to my world: Mr Laugh-A-Minute Greg, life and soul of the party, master of the quick one-liner, and a man who didn't know if or when the rollercoaster would ever stop. And if it did, would the walls slow down as well and let me see straight again?

I suppose the problem stems from the need to have people around me. I had married Dawn very young, and now we were going through a bitter divorce. Funnily enough, that's the one thing my drinking didn't really contribute to; she and I just fell out of love. None the less, the fact remained that I was living alone, going through a tough personal time, my Salford team weren't playing well, and I was facing up to it all in time honoured Andy Gregory fashion – through the bottom of a pint glass. It was all too easy to park the car after training and go straight across the road to the pub.

As ever, that is what I had done on this particular day, and I must admit there was a bit of a spring in my step as I looked forward to United lightening the gloom against Juve that evening. However, come kick-off time, it might as well have been a bog standard Monday afternoon for all I could remember about the match. That's when I decided that enough was enough and things had to change, or Lauren would just remember her dad as an old drunk who killed himself before he was 40. That was one shame I wasn't going to heap on her, although God knows there have been enough. As a player there were plenty of occasions when I wasn't around, through being on tour in Australia, or travelling to and from matches. And I am ashamed to admit that, for probably half the time I was there, I'd had a drink.

I remember one dreadful night, when we lived in Grappenhall near Warrington. Lauren had fallen ill during the evening, and nothing Dawn could do was having any effect. But I was hardly in any state to help after another day on the pop. Eventually we called the doctor and fortunately she was only suffering from a spot of flu – but I would have been no use to her whatever the problem. It would be bad enough if that had been the only time I had let my little girl down over the years. If only.

After Dawn and I split up there were any number of occasions when arrangements for me to collect Lauren went out of the window after a few too many. That first driving ban had swiftly been followed by another, and then when I got my licence back it was accompanied by a warning from the judge, who said that if ever I was caught again I would be spending six months inside. If anything was going to, that should have shaken me into realising what I was doing. Instead, all it did was lead to phone calls to Dawn, saying that I couldn't come and pick up Lauren. If I was supposed to collect her at one, by midday I'd be too far gone to get behind the wheel. And woe betide anyone who dared to suggest that I took it easy, at least until I had had something to eat.

Not that I would be rolling my sleeves up ready for a fight. I may have been willing to take on anyone on the pitch, but off it I have never been a trouble-maker. I know some people who get pissed and want to take on the world. Others turn into Casanova and want to knock off anything in a skirt. Me, I just wanted to drink and drink until it was time to go, and then I'd get home and fall asleep. Dawn herself would tell you that drink wasn't really that much of a factor in us splitting up, and I can honestly say that I have never been violent in it. In fact, the only one in any danger was me – from falling off a bar stool or walking into something.

But I will hold my hands up and say that there are plenty of folk I have let down. I couldn't count the number of people I have fallen out with and who have lost all respect for me over the years. Especially since I got the worst piece of advice that anyone has ever given me, from a mate who told me that Guinness was like a meal in itself.

To a serious drinker, that was indeed music to my ears. So much so that I would go for days without food, and only eat when the dizziness and pain from having nothing in my stomach to throw up became too much to bear.

I was never at the stage where I woke up in the morning desperate for a pint to go with my cornflakes. In fact, I have never been one for drinking at home full stop. But whereas in the past I'd go out for a drink if I fancied one, over the last few years it got to the stage where I had to be in the pub or I thought I was missing something.

First one in, last one out – that was Andy Greg. I never wanted to go home and then the next day I'd wake up and not remember being there at all. You don't know how embarrassing it is, walking back into the pub and having to ask someone what I did the night before. I just wish they had awarded medals for drinking. I won 20-odd as a player, but I would have picked up twice as many if they gave them for necking pints!

When I had the Bluebell in Newton-le-Willows, you could effectively write off two or three days a week. There were many times when I would speak to someone at nine o'clock in the morning, when I was just coming round from the night before, and make arrangements for later that day. Come six o'clock, a guy from the brewery or whoever it was would turn up, I would be fast asleep. When they got someone to wake me up, I wouldn't even remember having spoken to them earlier in the day. On other occasions I would sit there discussing things with reps or whoever at twelve o'clock having already had a few pints, and be talking absolute broken biscuits.

My whole world was a shambles, and if I hadn't needed the money because of my divorce I would have packed it in as coach of Salford 12 months earlier than I did. In fact, it was only on the advice of my bank that I decided to stick it out for a while. I may have had second thoughts if I had realised that certain people were going to stab me in the back – but more of that later. And despite the booze, I did put in a hell of a lot of work for that club, although I am ashamed to say that there were times when I turned up at the Willows the worse for wear as well. While it all ended in tears at Salford, I still have some bloody good friends at the club. None more so than Chris Brooks, the doctor, who pulled me aside one day and asked, 'Why are you doing this to yourself, Greg? You're self-destructing, and if you carry on you will soon be dead.'

The problem is, you think you are indestructible. Just like I used to think I was above the law – until I was hauled over, at least. That's why this is my third attempt at a book, following on from *Drink Driving – How To Get Away With It*, and *101 Ways to Cadge A Lift!*

As a player with Widnes, Warrington, Wigan and even Great Britain there were plenty of times when I'd have more than my share, but would run it off at training the next day. And before anyone points the finger at a particular stinker I may have had, I can say hand on heart that I never let the drink affect my performances on the pitch. If anything, the opposite was true. The night before Wigan played Halifax in the 1988 Challenge Cup final, I even had a couple of pints with Bill Hartley, our conditioner. We strolled into a pub down the road from where the team was staying, and a guy came over and asked me if I wasn't playing the next day, because he'd had a bet on me to win the Lance Todd Trophy as Man of the Match.

I told him I was, asked him how much he'd put on me and was told that he had bet a tenner. At the time I was at the peak of my form and had confidence to match. So I took another ten quid out of my pocket, told him to stick that on as well, and waltzed off with the Man of the Match award the following day.

The next year exactly the same thing happened. The night before we stuffed St Helens, Bill and I walked into the pub and the same bloke was there again. Once more he came over and said, 'I'm going to stick a tenner on you tomorrow, Andy.' This time, even though I was just as confident, I told him to keep his money in his pocket, because I didn't think I was likely to win a second Lance Todd Trophy – only one other player, Gerry Helme of Warrington, had ever done it. True enough, I had a blinder and should have won it, but Ellery Hanley got the vote instead – although I was back the following year to win a second award against Warrington.

That summer in 1988 I went on tour with Great Britain, and the night before each of the first two Tests we all stayed in our rooms – and duly got stuffed. Before the third Test in Sydney there was a knock on the door, and Phil Ford was standing there: 'Let's go for a pint,' he said. With the series already lost I didn't need a second invitation, so we joined the rest of the squad who weren't playing in the Kiwi bar, just down the road from the Manly Pacific Hotel. Myself, Phil and Mike Gregory – no relation, he's got less hair than me – had three pints of Guinness and got a good night's kip. The following day Fordy scored a brilliant solo try, Mike went the length of the field for another, and I was Man of the Match as we hammered a disbelieving Aussie side. Now I'm not putting it all down to the fact that we had a couple of drinks the night before, but I am saying that in those days it didn't affect me. Mind you, that was before I started putting away about 200 gallons of the stuff a day!

Anyway, back to reality – or at least what passed for it in those days. I had been thinking about sorting myself out for a while, but to a drinker tomorrow never comes. If it crossed my mind on Wednesday, I'd tell myself that I would get on the wagon by Thursday, and so on. But, this time, after that United match, I finally decided to get myself straight. I had already considered going to a health farm or seeing a medical expert, but I'd never had an agent, so I told myself this was something I had to do alone as well.

You can't imagine what a relief it was finally to come clean and get things off my chest. I started off by spilling the beans to the *Sun* – and despite what some people still think, I didn't get a penny for that story; it was just a case of opening my heart. I then went on a good head-clearing holiday to Gran Canaria with Howard Clegg and Neil Hilton, a couple of the Salford directors, and that did me the world of good. Not so much that it stopped me from going back this year and nearly killing myself in a drinking competition, mind: I thought I was necking two pints of Red Bull and vodka, which would have been bad enough, but someone had stitched me up and it was pure spirits. I was ill for three days. I have no doubts that there will be the odd time when I am pissed again – but not like before.

Every time anyone sees me with a drink now they nudge their mate and say, 'Oh aye, Greg's back on the pop, I see.' But I have never said and will never say, that I have kicked it into touch for good. The difference now is that I do it occasionally and on my terms, and not through force of habit.

But this is like starting a whole new life – one in which people aren't trying to shaft me left, right and centre. I have helped a lot of people out over the years, even when I was off my head, but there was never anyone to put their arm around my shoulder sand listen to my worries. Instead, there were plenty of people I classed as friends who just took advantage. Mates like coaches who were stabbing me in the back, or people who had their fingers in the till at the pub. Yet all of a sudden that has stopped, at the same time as my hard drinking. I have done a good enough job of shafting myself, without anyone else getting in on the act – but now my finger is on the pulse, I see everything differently.

I think there are lots of folk who see me differently as well. In fact, a few days after I had cut down on the booze, loads of people asked me if there was something wrong with my eyes. There are those who go for nose jobs, boob jobs or whatever – everyone thought I'd been for one on my eyes, because they were suddenly clear again, not red and half-closed. And it made a hell of a change to throw people out of the clubhouse, the next pub I had in Wigan, when they were abusive or started making trouble through drink. There have been plenty of times recently when I have listened to someone ranting and slurring their words and thought, 'Oh Christ, Andy, you were like that every night not so long ago.'

I have started watching a bit of television as well, although that is never going to be a compulsion for me. I have never been much of a telly addict, and couldn't tell you any of the characters from *Emmerdale*, *EastEnders* or whatever. I have always been interested in news programmes and sport shows – although in the past I used to watch them all in the pub. Nowadays, however, I am quite happy to sit at home with my feet up in front of the box for a couple of hours.

And I am well prepared for all the people who think that, because they see me with a pint in my hand I must have had another dozen to go with it. That is something I have lived with for the past 18 years. When I was at Widnes I was supposed to have been pissed in Wigan the night before a big game, and

Doug Laughton, my coach at the time, rang to tell me the rumours. He just said, 'I know you weren't, but if you ever do fancy a pint before a match, just make sure you go out of town to have it.' Then there was the time I was supposed to be involved in some drug scandal in Ashton.

My mum, Lois, is the only person who is totally against me having a drink – but then, she got divorced herself because of it, so she has every reason to be. She works in the middle of Wigan, and no one would ever tell her that they had seen her Andrew presenting trophies at a kids' awards night, or doing a coaching session for youngsters. But if she had a quid for every time she's heard someone say, 'Your Andrew was as drunk as a monkey in town last night,' she'd be a rich woman.

There was one occasion some years ago when things got out of hand, when I went with a few mates in a minibus to watch Liverpool play Arsenal. We all went back to Ashton for a drink afterwards, and when I was at the bar standing my round, two lads went behind my back and bought some drugs. I couldn't even tell you what they were, because I have never had any interest in that kind of thing, and I never will. But within a fortnight I got a call from my mum asking me what I thought I was doing, buying drugs in Ashton.

The simple truth is, if someone sees me with a coke, then in their eyes it must have a bacardi in it. A tonic has to be laced with gin, while an orange must be at least half vodka. If I've had two pints, it's a dozen by the time the rumour gets out – and I have fallen over, thrown up on the landlord and got chucked out of the pub. Sometimes I think I may as well have a shedful because that's the story which will do the rounds, whatever I do.

It is as though people think that, because I was a tough rugby player, and then I dealt with all these hard men as a coach, I mustn't have any feelings. Nothing could be further from the truth. There have been plenty of times when I have been really hurting inside, but I have had no one to talk to. Especially over the divorce and Lauren. Never mind the fact that it all ended in tears for me and Dawn. The fact is, she is the mother of my daughter, and a bloody good one at that. I will always have feelings for her even though we have both got separate lives to lead now.

That side of my life is over now, and I have finally realised that there is still plenty to look forward to – and I don't need to spend all day in the pub to enjoy it. Last orders for the Andy Gregory of old were have now been called.

TWO

From Banner Street to Banner Headlines

I guess I have always been a bit of an awkward sod – I think that's the reason why I was born in the front room of our house in Banner Street, Lower Ince in Wigan. Whether my mum planned that or not I don't know: judging from the way things went later in life, it was probably because I refused to arrive at the right time. On this occasion, though, I can honestly hold my hands up and say that I had very little choice in the matter.

My early memories certainly don't include my dad. He left home when I was very young, leaving Mum to bring up me, my older brother Neil and younger one Bryn with help from my gran and grandad, Edith and Harold. They were fantastic to us, and one of the best photos I've got is from my first Wembley final in 1981, of my grandad with the Challenge Cup. Without him and Edith, my mum would have struggled to find the time to work, and things would really have been tough then.

I reckon I must have been a nightmare for my mum when I was growing up – I don't suppose much has changed there, then – because I was always on the go. I was never a good sleeper, and in the early days I was a real screamer of a baby. In fact it's literally only over the last few months that I have been able to settle down and do something static like sit in front of the box. Back then I was always on edge: if I was asleep or out of the room I always used to think I was missing something. My mum could never plonk me in front of the telly and know I'd be happy watching something for an hour or so.

My childhood was spent watching either Wigan Athletic in the old Northern Premier League or the rugby team down at Central Park, and playing sport. In fact, in those days I was a fair old footballer, and I used to play for the Double Seven Youth Club with a certain Danny Wilson. Everyone knows how he went on to play for Sheffield Wednesday among others, and carve out a great career as a manager. But if you had asked Mr Dickens, our coach at the time, he'd have probably said that I had just as big a future in the game as Danny. I could do with his money now, I'll tell you that.

Away from there, I was usually down at the Britannia Bridge playing fields with a rugby ball under my arm. There was nothing else to do in those days: there were no computer games, no drug culture, no raves. That's one thing that worries me about Lauren growing up. You just don't hear kids talking about youth clubs, cubs or brownies any more. But she's got a great mum in Dawn, and there's no danger of her not knowing the difference between right and wrong.

When I was growing up, if you weren't playing sport there wasn't much to occupy the time at all. Believe it or not, I was also a choirboy for three years at St Mary's C of E – I still get to church every Sunday if I can – and I had a great time as a member of the Fourth Wigan Cub Scouts. But rugby was my main pastime from around the age of eight, although all the other lads were older and bigger than me. Not that being the smallest has ever bothered me. Even when I was lining up for Great Britain against the Aussies, I always knew I'd be the tiniest on the field. But fear is one thing at least that has never been a part of my life.

My first taste of team rugby came at Whelley Range Middle School, under Derek Birchall, who has remained a great friend to this day – although the Gregory stubborn streak had him tearing his hair out on more than one occasion. Such as the time he ended up threatening me with the pump if I didn't play rugby, I insisted on going swimming.

As you might guess, there was no doubting what I really wanted to do. However then, as now, the best way to get me to dig my heels in and be contrary was to tell me what to do. Although I was really starting to enjoy my rugby, when I moved on to Deanery High School I could never get a place in the town team.

There was a guy called Chris Ratchford who went to St Thomas More, and who captained Wigan, Lancashire and England Schools, while I wasn't even selected. He ended up signing for Wigan, but never played a professional game for them, while I – who couldn't hold a light to him as a schoolboy – went on to have a great career. That's why I always tell kids who get a bit downhearted after a few setbacks, never to give up. I've been there and done that, and you never know how it's going to turn out.

Academically, however, it was a different ball game. I was never any good at metalwork or woodwork or any of the usual 'boy-type' lessons. I think it was probably laziness as much as anything. The only subjects I excelled at were PE, religious studies and, believe it or not, cookery. In fact, I went on to become a qualified chef, as I'll explain later. And although my maths wasn't exactly Carol Vorderman standard, I picked up enough to know the difference between picking up £60 a week in the kitchens at Greater Universal Stores and taking home £150 working in Sammy Evans's scrapyard after I signed for Widnes.

Back on the subject of rugby, I joined the local amateur club Rose Bridge as a junior, but I remember Cliff Fleming, the president of Wigan St Patrick's, telling me I was wasting my time, and so I went off down to road to join them. That was probably as big a turning point in my life as any, because by the end of the following year I was the BARLA Player of the Season, in the Lancashire squad and dreaming of the big time.

Towards the end of my first full season at St Pat's we played Pilkingtons, our big rivals from St Helens. Although we lost 96–2, I had a great game, believe it or not. In the last minute, however, one guy made a break down the wing, and I tapped his ankles to stop him scoring and broke my wrist. It was the first serious injury of my life, but I was totally dedicated to the game then, and neither the fracture nor the nature of the defeat could keep me down for long.

I must have done enough to impress someone in that first season, because the following year I was chosen for the Possibles against the Probables, effectively a final trial game to decide the Lancashire county team. I was up against Ray Ashton, from Widnes St Marie's, who was ahead of me in the running for the scrum-half spot. We sat down afterwards and waited for the XIII to be read out, and I can still vividly remember sweating as they ran through the first six. When they came to number seven – Andy Gregory – it was all I could do to stop myself charging out of the dressing-room and shouting it out to everyone. Then again, I've never been the fastest of players, so they'd probably have caught me before I'd reached the door.

We played Cumbria and Yorkshire, and that led to a Great Britain call to face France at Castleford. Although we lost the game I was Man of the Match, and from that day onwards I had about 12 clubs pestering me to sign. It was the first time that anyone had shown an interest in asking me to turn pro, and although everyone in the amateur game wanted me to wait until after the BARLA tour to Australia at the end of the season, I decided that the time had come for me to chance my arm with the big boys.

THREE

The End of Life as a Pan Scrubber

I don't suppose I had the ideal grounding for life as a rugby player. After all, there can't be too many running around in Super League nowadays who have spent three years as a choirboy, washed women's hair in a salon on Saturdays, and then trained as a chef before turning pro. Yet that's exactly how it was with me.

I left school at 15 with only a couple of CSEs to my name and went straight to Great Universal Stores, in the Marsh Green area of Wigan, as a pan-washer. It wasn't the most glamorous of starts to anyone's working life, and a world away from my real ambition of becoming a chef. But I made some fantastic friends, people like Joe, my fellow pan-scrubber; Agnes, who worked on the chips and Mavis, a friend of the family who got me the job in the first place. Not that Joe was in any danger of suffering from scrubber's elbow: he was also the shop steward, and he spent a lot of his time on union business – leaving me with the muck and the grease!

After a while I enrolled at Bolton College, where I began studying to become a chef. The mornings were great, when we were making the food. But after we'd made it and eaten it, the thought of the theory classes in the afternoon was usually overtaken by the desire to nip off for a couple of pints with Geoff Dodge and Ste Clare. From there it was on to St Helens College, where I got the first stage of my City and Guilds – although, funnily enough, I didn't get any stick for being from Wigan. By then I had signed for Widnes, and I knew that was hard for the blokes on the course with me to accept at times. I was becoming a regular in the first team and working in Sammy Evans's scrapyard as well as trying to qualify as a chef, while for them the studies were the means to their entire livelihood. And unless you cracked a really big place, it wasn't the biggest earner in the world either. In fact I reckon the three worst paid professions are hairdressing – my mum still works in a salon – nursing, and being a chef. The day I signed for Widnes I virtually doubled my money, and that was before I'd even played a game for them.

But if things had worked out a little differently, I could easily have been pulling on the red shirt of Salford rather than the white of Widnes. Early on in my career at GUS, I had got a phone call from Albert White at Salford, asking me to go training at the Willows the following Tuesday. He picked me up in a taxi – very impressive for someone who was used to the bus – and took me down to the ground. The first session went well, and so two days later I was back again to meet Alex Murphy, who was the coach at the time. Albert told him, 'This is your scrum-half for tomorrow' – to which he got the reply, 'He's not very big, is he?'

Albert told Alex not to worry about that, but to concern himself with the rest of the team. It didn't sink in with me as to what he was getting at. After all, even though Salford were going through a lean spell, they were still the glamour club of the day, with great international players such as David Watkins, Keith Fielding, Colin Dixon and Steve Nash. In fact, it was only when I thought of Nashie that it hit home to me. He couldn't play in the Friday game against Barrow because he was on international duty – and that left me to make my début after just two training sessions. Murphy said to me, 'Make sure you're here for six o'clock tomorrow night,' and that was that. At that stage I didn't even know who we were playing.

I went to work as usual the next day, and when I came home my gran had made me a huge steak and egg sandwich – to beef me up, as she put it. Then mum, Derek Birchall, Cliff Fleming and I all headed off to the Willows for my big night. Nothing could have prepared me for that. In the dressing-room all the shirts were laid out in numerical order, and I was next to prop-forward Mike Coulman. I looked up, and his legs were almost as tall as me. That was the first time I thought, 'What am I doing here?' – but not the last. I was never short of belief in my own ability, but as we came out of the tunnel I can still recall looking across at Phil Hogan, who was the subject of a record transfer deal when he joined Hull KR; Jimmy Nulty, my opposite number; and, worst of all, Eddie Szymala, who was an absolute monster, a huge skinhead covered from head to foot in tattoos. For a young lad who looked like he should have been in bed by kick-off time, that was an eye-opener, believe me.

Things started well, and with my first touch I made a bit of a break – only to come crashing down to earth when Hogan tackled me and whispered in my ear, 'That's the last time you'll be doing that tonight, son.'

Come half-time we were heading for defeat, although I knew I wasn't doing too badly. That's when I got my first taste of what being a professional was really all about. Back in the dressing-room, Murphy sent all the forwards up to one end – the Salford sheds aren't the biggest in the game by any means – and absolutely tore into them. I was at the end of the row of backs, and he pointed at me and roared, 'He's given his all for this team tonight. You lot? I should banjo the lot of you.' I don't know if that was some sort of psychology designed to make me feel good, but I remember thinking 'My God, we don't have anything like this at St Pat's.'

It must have done the trick, though, because we went on to win the game quite easily. The only thing that marred it for me came when Colin Dixon put me through a gap with about five minutes to go. There was no one near me, the line was wide open . . . and I knocked on. Even so, I still won the Man of the Match award. But since I hadn't signed for Salford, I was down in the programme as A.N. Other. Only no one remembered to tell the PA announcer. As I walked off, he bellowed down the microphone: 'Tonight's Man of the Match award goes to A.N. Other – and for anyone who wants to know, that's Andy Gregory from Wigan.'

Murphy immediately jumped up in the dug-out, cracked his head open on the roof and went storming into the announcer's office. He got hold of him and was going so wild that I half-expected the poor bloke to come flying through the window. Still, I don't suppose he ever made the same mistake again while Murph was coach.

I got £50 for being named Man of the Match, and put it back into the players' pool. It was the first time in my life that I'd ever got any serious money for playing rugby league, and I ended up giving it away. But to someone who had visions of cracking the big time, what the hell.

As I left the ground Murphy, Brian Snape the chairman and the rest of the board told me that they'd have a meeting the following Tuesday to come up with a deal for me to sign up to. But over that weekend my dad got wind of the fact that I'd played for Salford, and decided to make a reappearance to assist with negotiations. My dad had spent nine years as a pro at the Willows, but hadn't left on the best of terms, so in hindsight maybe he wasn't the best person to conduct talks on my behalf. They offered me £1,500 to sign, he insisted on £2,000, and when they refused to budge a few harsh words and home truths came out from both sides. The upshot was that I ended up walking away and going back to playing as an amateur with St Pat's.

Not that there was anything wrong – or less enjoyable – in that. But while I seemed to be earning a big reputation in certain quarters, there were others where I definitely wasn't considered to be the business. And I can still recall one comment as clearly as if it was yesterday. It came after we'd beaten Oldham St Anne's, and I had won the Man of the Match award again. I was queueing up at the bar in the clubhouse with everyone else when I heard one Wiganer say to Jack Keen, the chief scout at Central Park: 'Isn't it about time you signed this Gregory – he's the best thing to come out of St Pat's for years.' Jack would never admit his answer, but I remember it vividly. He said: 'We've had him watched and he's not a bad 'un, but he'll never be big enough or good enough.'

I suppose it could have broken me, hearing someone from my hometown club effectively writing off my chances of ever making it with one of the biggest names in the world. As far as I was concerned, though, I simply thought: 'Well, I won't be going to Wigan, then – I'll just have to become the best in the business somewhere else.' And, unknown to me, that somewhere else was just around the corner.

FOUR

A Family at War

My mum is probably the most honest person I know. And that led to one almighty bust-up when I finally decided to take the plunge and accept one of the offers to sign professional that had started to flood into the Gregory household.

She was very good friends with a Wigan director called Arthur Stone, and during one conversation she had virtually promised him that when I did turn pro, it would be at Central Park. That, of course, was without the benefit of knowing that the chief scout had already written off my chances of cracking the big time. The other thing that was swaying me away from my hometown club was the fact that, in those days, the only place Wigan were heading was the Second Division. Widnes, on the other hand, were rapidly establishing themselves as the top team in the business.

I was still playing for St Pat's and my big break came in a game against Widnes St Marie's and my old rival Ray Ashton. Widnes coach Doug Laughton came along to watch the match with his right-hand man, Harry Dawson, with a view to signing Ray. I just happened to be on the other side in what was a very tight match, and in the last minute I threw out one of the passes of my life to the winger, who caught it and dived over in the corner to clinch victory. Doug immediately turned to Dawson and said, 'Forget about Ray Ashton, that Wigan half-back can play, and he's the one we're getting.'

By then I had already made my own mind up – as I said, I was a stubborn so-and-so at the best of times – that Widnes was a big enough club for the Gregory talents. So Doug and Harry didn't have a great deal of persuading to do when they came round to the house to try to sign me. But that was where the problems started with my mum. She was in the kitchen making a pot of tea when I put pen to paper in the lounge. You can imagine how well that went down. So much so that when the two of them had left, she tore up my signing-on cheque for £2,000, at a time when we didn't exactly have money coming out of our ears. But we had a bit of a natter, for want of a better word and, eventually, she came round to the idea that Wigan wasn't the club for me.

The Widnes scrum-half at the time was a guy called Reg Bowden, who was a great player, but I had enough confidence in my own ability to believe that I could take his place in the side. Doug had never been afraid to blood up-and-coming youngsters, and lads like Eric Hughes, Stuart Wright, Mick Adams and Mick Burke had all got their first chance under his regime. My immediate interest, however, was a trip to Wembley just one week after I'd joined them. Part of my signing-on deal was two tickets to see Widnes play Wakefield Trinity in the 1979 Challenge Cup final, so off I went with Jimmy Taylor, a big mate of mine who had never been down before.

The funny thing was that people around Wigan and St Helens

were still asking me if I had made my mind up about who I'd join. I had already signed for Widnes at the time but – unlike certain other incidents in the future – I wasn't exactly big news. There was no big press conference, no newspaper headlines, just the back door opening wide enough to let a little unknown 17-year-old slip through. But my main concern was to put the record straight and earn a few headlines through my playing abilities – and as far as I saw it, a decent pre-season and a few good A team games would soon see me realise my dream.

Fair enough, I had a few games for the reserves in that 1979–80 season and everyone was pushing Dougie to play me. But, unknown to me, he had a stubborn streak to rival my own, and his response to all the pressure was to sign Johnny Taylor from Leigh, and put him ahead of me in the pecking order. If that wasn't bad enough, I had already had to fight back from another broken wrist, courtesy of my old mate John Stockley. I had made a break down the wing, but when I looked to pass John, like he often did, was day-dreaming and nowhere in sight. I had no choice but to take the tackle, fell awkwardly, and ended up in Accident and Emergency again. Two games after coming back from that, I went over on my ankle and broke a bone in my foot. To say it got me down was an understatement, and I spent a couple of hours in the waiting room at Broad Green hospital wondering whether I should even bother trying to make it, or concentrate on earning a crust as a chef.

In the end there was no real choice too make, and I fought my way back once more, only for Doug to sign Taylor. By doing so he earned himself a visit from yours truly, armed with the first transfer request of my career. He told me, 'I know you want to go to Wigan, so fair enough. I'll let you go, but I can guarantee that within a week you'll wish you were back with us.' That was enough for me, especially when I looked at the league tables, which showed Wigan battling (unsuccessfully, as it turned out) against relegation. So I decided to stay put. In hindsight Doug did me a massive favour, because there was no way I would have been given the time to develop in a poor Wigan side under pressure for results.

I finally got my chance as a substitute against Huddersfield, when I came on after the break and made three or four tries in the second half. Maurice Bamford, the Huddersfield coach, told Dougie that he had found a 'good 'un', as he put it. I think Laughton knew it – but there was no way he'd ever let on to me. I got a fair old hint, though, when he finally plonked me in from the start, and I was never out of the side again. There can't have been many players who have enjoyed such a fantastic start to life in the first team, and I ended that 1980–81 season by playing at Wembley in the Challenge Cup final.

The first of my eight Wembley finals is still the one my mum remembers most clearly, not least because of the journey down to London. She sat down on the train opposite Denis Law, and after a while plucked up courage to talk to him. He said he was heading to London, and she told him she was off to the Cup final to support Widnes. He immediately replied, 'That Andy Gregory's a good player,' and she was as proud as punch to be able to tell him I was her son. They chatted all the way down, and it turned out he followed rugby league closely and knew a lot about me. My mum couldn't believe it, and neither could I when she told me. Here was Denis Law, one of Manchester United's all-time greats, talking in glowing terms about a young Wigan lad playing for Widnes. For a United fan that was almost as good as the match itself, and my mum still remembers it. In fact, that made her weekend more than the game – even if it did signal the arrival of her middle son on the biggest stage of all, in front of millions of viewers all over the world.

FIVE

The Whole Tooth about Wembley

There haven't been too many things in my life which have left me shaking with nerves and sweating with fear. But a visit to the dentist is one that is guaranteed to get the butterflies fluttering and make the hands all clammy. So when I was building up to my first trip to Wembley as a player in 1981, the last thing I needed was the worst bout of toothache I'd ever suffered. It had all started a couple of weeks before we were due to face Hull KR in the final, but I had assumed that it was something to do with the big game coming up and thought nothing of it. Big mistake.

We travelled to London on the Wednesday before the match, and I remember Dougie taking us all down the pub. I was only on orange at the time – yes, I haven't always liked a drink – but he insisted I had a couple of pints to help me sleep in the belief that I'd be too nervous to rest properly before Saturday. Little did he know how true that would prove for me in the last few hours before the game.

By Friday the tooth had really got quite bad, and come the eve of the final I had to get some painkillers from the doctor. By one o'clock in the morning it had become unbearable – not that I got too much sympathy from my room-mate, Keith Elwell, who was dead to the world. He was so tight he wouldn't give anything away, even a couple of hours' kip!

I knocked up the doctor, and within half an hour we were both in a taxi heading for the hospital. As we walked in, both in Widnes tracksuits, a couple of Rovers fans spotted me; they must have thought their boys were in for a field day, as the opposition scrum-half was hardly getting the best preparation for the match. I had the tooth taken out and a gauze put over the wound. The main thing was that the pain had gone, and I was just left with a big hole in my mouth.

From that moment it was all about Wembley, and I remember feeling very worried about whether my mum had got there okay as we were walking out of the tunnel. The actual enormity of the occasion didn't seem to hit me at all, and when the game started I thought I'd escaped the dreaded Wembley nerves. But then we had a scrum near our own line, and the black-and-white of Widnes and red-and-white of Hull KR suddenly took over everything. I was in a world of my own for a couple of seconds, until Mick Adams whacked me on the back of the head and said, 'We'll have a bloody good look around later. Keep your head down for 80 minutes, Greg.'

It certainly did the trick. I was scared to death of dropping my concentration again, not in case I gave a chance to Hull KR, but because of what Mick would do to me if I did. Come half-time we were winning without playing particularly well, and Dougie got us all in the changing-room to tell us where we were going wrong. He did a head count and noticed Keith Elwell was missing. He asked where 'Chiefy' was – remember, this was half-time in the biggest game on the rugby league calendar – and Mick Adams, quick as a flash, replied: 'You know it's his testimonial . . . well, he's going round the crowd with a bucket.' The whole changing-room fell about, and the crowd must have wondered what the hell was going on when we emerged for the second half with huge grins on our faces.

What followed was the best moment of my career. I got the ball three minutes after the restart, stepped past Paul Harkin and Steve Hubbard and scored under the sticks. It might not have been the best try ever scored at Wembley – but this was my début at the great stadium, and no one was ever going to tell me otherwise at the time. Straight from the kick-off I caught the ball again, and Len Casey let me know what he thought of my try with an elbow to the face. That was the last I saw of the gauze which had covered the hole where my tooth had been. I picked myself up just in time to see Mick Burke kick two more points and send us even closer to our eventual 18–9 win.

A couple of days later, brother Bryn asked me what it had all been like, and I honestly couldn't remember that much – probably less then than now. So I told him, 'I'll just have to go back and do it all again.'

Around Widnes I was the big hero, and everyone was talking about my night in hospital with toothache. Even Keith Elwell was getting in on the act: when he was asked for his version of the story, he said he'd never been so tired for a game, as he hardly got a wink of sleep for looking after me. He must have been after the sympathy vote to get a few quid more for his testimonial!

Next season, 1981–82, I was a fixture in the Widnes side, and I even won two Great Britain caps against France in December, at Hull and Marseilles, before finishing the season at Wembley again. This time we were up against Hull FC, and we came back in the last couple of minutes to draw 14–14. Sadly all that was to no avail, as Hull pipped us in the replay at Elland Road – although I took some pleasure in setting up a try for Stuart Wright, who lots of people said was soft but is a man I'd rate among the top three wingers I've ever played with.

To make matters worse, I didn't make the Great Britain side for the first two Tests against Australia later that autumn, when they absolutely stuffed us. I finally got my chance against the old enemy in the third match at Headingley, and for 60 minutes we were equal to them before Wayne Pearce ran in a hat-trick to take them clear at 32–8. The 1982–83 season was a bit run of the mill, even though we finished it off by winning the Premiership Trophy at Leeds, but in 1984 we were back at Wembley to face Wigan. They were heading back to the top by then, but were undone in the final by a couple of great tries by Joe Lydon – another who had snubbed his hometown club to come to Naughton Park.

The best thing about that match for me was the form of our prop, Kevin Tamati. He had really struggled to find his best form for Widnes, and they were very close to sending him back home to New Zealand, so he couldn't have picked a better time to turn it on. Kevin spent most of the build-up to the game trying to teach me an old Maori insult. I can't remember the word, but it meant 'White New Zealander', and he assured me it would knock Wigan's Graeme West, another Kiwi, right off his game. Westie was really giving me stick from the off, but when I bellowed this word at him it knocked him right off his game for a while, and Kevin nearly collapsed laughing.

The only disappointment of the day for me was the reaction of the Wigan fans, who accused me and Joe of making obscene gestures to them after the match. True, Wigan was our hometown club, but we really wanted to beat them – after all, if I was up against Bryn in the final I'd do anything I could to win. But allegations of that sort were way out of order, petty, sour grapes because two Wiganers had won the Cup for another side.

There's nothing like the next game to bring you crashing down to earth, and I certainly landed with a bump when I headed to Australia with the 1984 Great Britain tour party as the best scrum-half in the country. I had an absolute nightmare on the trip. We lost all three Tests against the Kangaroos, and I got sick of seeing headlines about how useless the little Pommie was. Things picked up a bit for me in New Zealand, where I was Man of the Match in two of the three Tests, even though we were whitewashed there as well.

That was also the trip when I made what must rank as one of the worst decisions of my career. I had been at loggerheads with Kiwi prop Kurt Sorensen throughout the first match of that series, and in the second Test in Wellington I finally cracked and broke his nose with an absolute pearler of a punch. He spent the next ten years chasing me all over the fields of England and New Zealand trying to get revenge – although on one occasion he proved what a genuine bloke he is. It came when I was with Wigan and he was at Widnes, and I got sent off against them for the second year running by referee Colin Morris for alleged biting and gouging. Remember, Kurt and I had stood toe to toe for a decade, but he sent a letter to the Rugby Football League on my behalf, and it saved me from a lengthy ban. Quite rightly so, as well: I hadn't bitten him – I'd just stood on his head instead.

Back on the tour we still had the Papua New Guinea leg to go, and by then all we wanted to do was get home. We were 6–0 down in the Tests, morale was rock bottom, and every day it seemed that someone else was going home with one injury or another. In fact, the only person who loved the last stage was Castleford hooker Kevin Beardmore – because we couldn't get him off the hotel roof. He'd pop down for training, and came down for the match itself, but spent the rest of his time in PNG sunbathing. He came back to England looking like one of the natives. At least we managed to beat the Kumuls, so our Test record wasn't a complete blank. But for me it remains one of the worst times of my career. In 17 weeks away from home we had won just one of seven internationals, and I'd played terribly in the only bit that really counted, against the Aussies.

I suppose it wasn't a complete flop, though. I was sharing a room with Mike Smith, the Hull KR stand-off, and by the end of the trip I knew the words to 'Red, Red Robin' inside out. After over three months listening to him sing the bloody thing, I still have to go out of the room if ever I hear it.

SIX

Goodbye to Widnes, Hiya to the Wire

By the time I came back off that 1984 tour I was well established as the best scrum-half in England. I was also out of contract at Widnes. In those days you didn't sign up for a certain amount of years, it was a case of fulfilling certain terms and conditions along the way. In return you got your signing-on fee, and then you got bonuses for things like making the first team, playing for Lancashire, England or Great Britain – and I had achieved everything in just over three years. That left me playing for match payments alone, and as far as I was concerned, it wasn't enough. If I'd got a tenner for every time I asked the committee for a new contract, I wouldn't have needed one – I'd have been that rich. But on each occasion I asked, they flatly refused. Cue the Gregory stubborn streak once again.

I put my head down in pre-season training, won the Man of the Match award in our first game at Warrington . . . and promptly disappeared. The next day I picked up all the papers – which made me the headline news for my performance – and headed for Manchester Airport with Dawn to catch a flight to Malta. I didn't tell a soul where I was going, and no one could find me. In fact, the only guy I spoke to about it was the customs officer who checked my passport on the way home, who said, 'Jesus, you're in some trouble, aren't you, mate?' By then I was adamant that I had played my last game for Widnes but – surprise, surprise – they suddenly wanted to talk turkey with me.

When it came to digging your heels in, I was the champion. There was only one guy who ever ran me close, and that was Paul Woods, a scrum-half who played for Widnes, Hull and Wales. His determination knew no bounds, so much so that he almost got us banned from one Widnes pub during the build-up to one particular match. Paul, Mick Adams and I had gone to West Bank for a game of pool, and Woodsy was beating everyone. He must have won about ten on the trot by the time someone got the better of him. Paul's answer was simple: he said, 'I'm not losing another', and promptly snapped every single cue in the place to prove his point.

Widnes still expected me to go back to them, but I was having none of it. A lot of clubs were offering money for me, but I was holding out because I wanted to go to Wigan. After I hadn't played for four months Widnes eventually realised they should cash in, and as Challenge Cup deadline day loomed they finally agreed to sell me. That's when I got a phone call out of the blue from Maurice Lindsay at Wigan. He told me that although Wigan had offered the most money, Widnes had insisted they would never sell me to them, simply because they knew it was the one club I wanted to join. That left me facing the entire season on the sidelines, until I got another call on the Sunday night, just hours before the transfer deadline expired, from Warrington coach Reg Bowden. He told me the harsh reality of the situation: if I didn't put pen to paper quickly, no club would pay a transfer fee for me because they wouldn't be able to play me in the Cup. I'd be out then for the rest of the year, and by next season who knows if anyone would come in.

First thing in the morning I was signing on at Wilderspool and I have to say that I loved just about all of it at Warrington. Some people have slagged me off since and said that my heart wasn't in it, but nothing could be further from the truth. If that had been the case, how come they voted me Player of the Year in 1985? Some of my greatest games were in a Warrington shirt – like the day I sent Mark Roberts in for four tries as we put 50-odd on Leeds at Headingley. In fact, it was going so well that I'd shelved all thoughts of going to Wigan, until Tony Barrow took over as coach in March 1986.

Nowadays Tony and I get on great, but back then we never saw eye to eye. I used to spend his team talks in the changing-room toilets, and it didn't help that he was a big fan of a young scrum-half on the books at the time called Paul Bishop. From the moment he took charge, I guess it was only a matter of time before I left.

There were some memorable moments along the way, though, starting with my début when I was Man of the Match again as we beat Bradford. That night I went into the middle of Warrington to celebrate with Mark Forster, his wife Gaynor, and Dawn. The girls went to the toilet at one stage of the evening, and a couple of lads grabbed their backsides. On their way back a bit of a row started, and the girls had beer thrown all over them. Mark and I went over to see what the noise was, and it all ended up in a massive fight. The police were called, and I finished the evening in the cells. One officer came in to see me, and I asked him if he was married. When he said he was, I asked what he'd have done in similar circumstances. He told me, 'Probably the same as you, Andy.' All charges were promptly dropped.

Then there was the Lancashire Cup final against Wigan in 1985, when I got sent off for trying to stamp on Nick du Toit's head. We were losing something like 34–6 at the time, and there were about three minutes left. I escaped a ban because the disciplinary hearing believed me when I said it was all an accident, I was rushing to get on with it as I still felt we had a chance of winning.

We ended that 1985–86 season by winning the Premiership Trophy at Elland Road with a great display against Halifax. But there was disappointment ahead for me later that autumn, when Deryck Fox got the Great Britain scrum-half job in the first Test against Australia. Everyone had thought I was a certainty for selection. I watched that match in a pub in the middle of Warrington with Bob Eccles, one of my team-mates, and Britain got thrashed. He consoled me by insisting that at least it made me even more certain to be selected for the next Test. But as we moved on to another pub, a fan greeted me with the news that coach Maurice Bamford had already announced from the dressing-room that he was sticking with the same team for the following game. Cue a few drinks. I finally got my chance in the third Test at Wigan, when Garry Schofield scored two tries and we pushed them all the way. But, typical of our luck, the turning point came when Kangaroo skipper Wally Lewis put a kick in on the seventh tackle, and the referee gave an obstruction try which has to rank as one of the worst decisions I've seen – and that was that.

Next season, 1986–87, the writing on the wall couldn't have

been in bigger capitals. Tony Barrow started to leave me out in favour of Paul Bishop, even though I knew full well that I was a better player than him. By then Wigan had got wind of the fact that all was not rosy; they spoke to me about a move, and this time I was determined to join them. I asked the Warrington board if they'd be prepared to sell me, and I think they were quite relieved. I reckon they were getting a bit fed up with me by then, because when I wanted to be awkward I could win gold medals in it. I had an official appointment to see them at a board meeting, and they told me to put my request in writing. So I nipped into the Touchdown Club, scribbled it on a beer mat, went back in and threw it on the table. As I turned round to walk out, they said, 'Permission granted – you're on the list at £125,000.'

I was a bit worried that the fee might be too big and would scare Wigan away. But Jack Robinson was doing the deal for them and he reassured me that they wouldn't back off. You wouldn't believe how good that sounded to me. Within a couple of weeks I was a Wigan player, and about to embark on the most glorious chapter of my rugby league life.

SEVEN

The Hometown Hero – At Last!

As soon as I heard that Wigan were interested in signing me it was clear that St Helens, who were also chasing me, didn't have a prayer. Alex Murphy, the Saints coach at the time, found this out halfway through a match he was summarising for the BBC one Saturday afternoon.

I was still a Warrington player at the time, but wasn't getting a run, so I was watching their game – against Wigan, of all teams – at home in Grappenhall when the telephone went during the half-time break. It was Alex on the line, desperate to know if I was going to Knowsley Road. I just said, 'I'm sorry, Murph, but I am going to have to let you down – I'm going to Wigan.' You could hear the disappointment in his voice, and I'm sure he was even more vitriolic in his second-half comments after that.

The next day I met Jack Robinson, who was acting on behalf of the Wigan board, and signed for a then world-record fee of

£130,000. Almost as soon as I'd put pen to paper, Jack presented me with a brown paper bag which contained 'a few quid up front'. And that nearly came back to haunt me a couple of years later. Ellery Hanley, Dean Bell and I were the highest earners at Wigan at the time, and one day the dreaded VAT man asked us if we had ever received any cash payments from the club. We said we had, but we presumed that Wigan had paid the tax on it. They seemed to be happy with it, and we all had chairman Maurice Lindsay to thank for resolving it for us – but it was a hairy moment, believe me.

On the playing side, I didn't get off to the most auspicious of starts. Wigan were building a great side, with the likes of Ellery, Dean, Shaun Edwards and co., and were hot favourites to reach Wembley in 1987 and give the club only its second Challenge Cup win since 1965. So a first-round trip to Oldham apparently posed no threat whatsoever to the mighty Central Park boys. But obviously no one had told the home team's scrum-half Paddy Kirwan, because with a couple of minutes left he dived over in the corner. Mick Burke – my old mate from the Widnes days – added the conversion, and that was that. Shock of the season, Wigan out, and no return to Wembley.

At least the season ended on a high, both for Wigan and for me personally, because I scored probably the best try of my career at Halifax to win the league. I was never the fastest man in the world, and you wouldn't have put money on me going anywhere when I got the ball on halfway. But I dummied half the Halifax team, most of the Wigan side, the ref and a touch judge to score under the posts. It was just a good job we were playing downhill, or I'd still be running. When I won the Lance Todd Trophy at Wembley the following season, they replayed that try at the official presentation dinner. I think they started the tape before the starters arrived, and I had just scored it by the time most people received their coffee.

That 1987-88 season was also memorable as the year we got a five-grand bonus for keeping our mouths shut. There had been no slip-ups on the road this time, and we were due to play holders Halifax at Wembley. Ellery, Dean and I were sent in to negotiate a bonus with the board on the Monday of final week – with express orders not to come out unless or until they agreed to cough up £3,000 a man for winning. Ellery was going to do the talking, but he never got the chance. As soon as we went in, the board told us what a big day it was for the town, and how it would prove the making of the club – so would £5,000 a player be acceptable? We all just about managed an open-mouthed nod, before scrambling out of the door.

We went back to the rest of the team who were waiting in the dressing-room, and I told them 'I'm sorry, lads, we haven't got the money we were after.' I don't know if they were more annoyed with us or the board – until I added: 'We've got five grand a man instead.' Inside 30 seconds every player was changed, boots on and out on the pitch, ready for training.

Our performance in that Challenge Cup final is probably the best that any side had played at Wembley in 20 years. Every move we called came off, every kick was inch-perfect and never mind beating Halifax, on that day I think we'd have done any club side in the world. And it was extra-special for me because I also picked up my first Lance Todd Trophy as well.

That year, 1988, was the start of almost a decade of total dominance by Wigan. For the next few years we were pretty much untouchable – although things were not always as harmonious off the field as on it. Ellery, Shaun Edwards and I may have had a telepathic understanding at times, but I didn't really see eye to eye with either of them. Ellery and Andy Goodway always used to have a bet at the start of the season over who'd score the most tries, and it would really piss me off.

I was usually the one who put them through the gaps to score, and I was the one who ended up dumped on his backside while they went under the posts. One year Andy got about 38 tries, and not a finger was laid on him for 36 of them – while 30 yards out I'd be sitting on my arse having been flattened.

One day at Wakefield I decided enough was enough, and when we were 60-odd points up I went out in the centres. Remember, I used to call every move, and the players and coaching staff were all screaming at me to get back in the middle. After ten minutes or so I made my way back, and when coach Graham Lowe asked me after the game what I had thought I was doing, I told him, 'If it's that easy to score tries, let the others put me through the gaps.' I got a bit more respect after that.

But there was no time to let internal rows get in the way. Everyone else hated us, so when it came to rugby, it was all for one, one for all. We were the Liverpool of the 1980s, the Manchester United of the 1990s: they all wanted to beat us, but very few managed it. We had internationals in just about every position – and all of them strong characters to boot. But when it came to being stubborn, I still reckon I was in a league of my own, even though Ellery and Shaun both had their run-ins with Graham Lowe as well.

My own came in 1989, when the coach decided that he'd like to play a squad system with me at scrum-half for half the game, and Shaun there for the rest. Everyone could see it was rubbish, but when he brought it up with me I told him, 'If you don't want me for 80 minutes, I won't play at all,' and walked off the training field. The board, the players and the fans all wanted me back, and I told Maurice Lindsay I'd come back if Lowe rang me. That day duly arrived when I was working at the scrapyard, and Tony Karalius answered the phone. I shouted to Tony, 'Tell him I'm out' – and Graham would have heard it, because I yelled it loud enough. That was my stubborn streak coming out again. But in the end Graham got hold of me, we shook hands, and he brought me back as a substitute in the John Player Special Trophy final – when I came on in the second half to put Ellery through a gap for the winner against Widnes.

The difference between Lowe and his successor John Monie was that John would always listen to you. If he fancied a new move and you didn't, he'd give it a go in training, but if it became clear that it was too complex or unworkable, he'd scrap it immediately. With the exception of one in the run-up to our 1989 Challenge Cup final against St Helens: John wanted Shaun to take a quick tap and kick the ball over his head for the others to run on to, in a move called 'St Helens'. But Shaun wouldn't have any of it and refused point blank, saying he wasn't about to make a fool of himself in front of 90,000 people and the millions watching on TV. Things were getting quite heated until I stepped in, did the move, and everyone was happy. A few of the lads came up after the session and thanked me for defusing a row that could have wrecked our Wembley build-up. I just replied: 'Who calls the moves? Me. And you won't be bloody hearing me call that one on Saturday.'

Not that we needed it, as we stuffed Saints 27–0. That was the game when a young Gary Connolly was at full-back for them – and was ruined before we even got on to the field. As the two teams lined up in the tunnel he was standing just behind Ellery, and Hanley was bellowing at him, about how Wigan were going to hammer him with kicks, and how he'd be crying to come off as soon as he could. Even a few of the older heads were a bit taken aback, because Ellery wasn't exactly whispering. The poor lad was destroyed before he even got to meet the dignitaries; he had a nightmare, and we strolled it.

The following season we were back at Wembley again, to beat Warrington and win another double. It was double time for me, too, as I picked up the Lance Todd Trophy for a second time. But, for me, one of the most memorable incidents in the match came when Joe Lydon flattened Paul Bishop. He had never been my favourite player from our days together at Warrington, and I could never work out how someone born in St Helens could have such a dodgy Aussie accent. Anyway, Joe cleaned him out with one of the best hits I've ever seen – and it couldn't have happened to a nicer bloke.

That was the game when Shaun played on for about an hour with a fractured eye socket. But while everyone else was fussing about it after the game, I don't think anyone in the Wigan side ever asked him how it was. It wasn't that we didn't care; it was just that we were so professional and focused that we didn't give it a second thought. In fact, we were such perfectionists that people would often be on the point of coming to blows in training, just for a dropped ball or a dodgy pass.

And there was the fact that we all accepted injuries as part of the job. In fact, for the last six years of my career, I don't think I ever played when I was 100 per cent fit. I spent so much time in a London clinic in the 1990–91 season that it's surprising I didn't pick up a Cockney accent. I was down there every week with Ellery, trying to get fit for Wembley, and training with Stewart Robson, the old Arsenal and West Ham footballer, and Daley Thompson. I used to leave Runcorn Station at six o'clock on a Monday morning, not train with the lads until I got back on the Saturday, play the game on Sunday, and then head down south again the following day. I did that for weeks, and it paid off when we won the league with a staggering run-in of eight games in nineteen days.

At the end of it all we had Wembley, against Saints again, with

Ellery and I both needing late fitness tests. I was okay, after a couple of cortisone injections to make sure, but Ellery's test was literally half an hour before the game. I asked the club medic Dr Zaman if he'd make it, and he said: 'He should do, he's had half a dozen jabs – he won't feel his leg all afternoon.' Ellery played that final more or less on one leg, but it was just the physical presence of the pair of us out on the pitch that counted. Sure enough we won again, although this time they did get within five points of us – and there was further satisfaction in the fact that Paul Bishop finished on the losing side once more!

We were back at our second home again in 1992, this time beating Castleford. But, for me, it was a bit of an anticlimax because Lee Crooks came into a tackle with his knees, gave me a dead leg, and put paid to my hopes of a third Man of the Match trophy. Not that I'm having a go at Lee – we all did whatever we could to help our side win, and that sort of thing was an accepted part of the game. I just wish someone else had got him first!

And being targeted by the opposition was hardly a new experience for me. When I moved to Salford Linda Atherton, our physio, overheard the Bradford coach Peter Fox telling his team that if they stopped 'that big headed so and so Gregory from playing, they'd stop us as well'. She told me what had gone on and warned: 'I think you'd better be careful, Andy, he's sending them all out looking for you.' I just told her: 'Linda, they've been trying it for 20 years and I'm still here, so one more won't make a difference.'

None the less, that injury was still a sour way to end my Wembley career – although I couldn't really complain because we'd cleaned up again throughout the season. At that moment in time, leaving Wigan was certainly the furthest thing from my mind. As far as I was concerned I would see out my career at Central Park. Little did I know that the Castleford final would be the last game I ever played for the club.

EIGHT

This Was Your Life

I have never had an agent throughout my career, either as a player or a coach. Maybe if I had, things wouldn't have ended on such a sour note at Wigan. But then again, contract negotiations at Central Park had never been a problem. I'd go in, reach an agreement with Maurice Lindsay, and three months later sign the deal. Maurice and I trusted each other implicitly, and there had never been any cause for either of us to doubt that trust. But when Maurice left to take over as chief executive of the Rugby Football League in 1992, things took a definite turn for the worst.

I had just come back early from Great Britain's tour to Australia, which had been an absolute nightmare for me. I had a groin injury, but the tour management had effectively forced me to play. I was having a terrible time, so much so that by the time my injury flared up again they were glad that I had to call it a day and head back home. I consoled myself with the fact that at least I could look forward to signing a new deal with Wigan. I had agreed one with Maurice before the tour departed and he had left the club, and all that remained was to tie up a few loose ends with Jack Robinson, who had taken over as chairman. But when I met Jack at the Lord Daresbury Hotel, just outside Warrington, to conclude things, he went back on the deal. He wanted me to take a drop in wages, which was bad enough. But the turning point came when he said: 'You're a Wigan lad, you'll never leave this club.' From the second he uttered those words, I knew I was going to move on. I signed for my old Widnes boss Doug Laughton, who was now in charge at Leeds – and lost the chance of appearing on *This Is Your Life* into the bargain.

Maurice had been on the phone to my mum a few months earlier, asking about my schoolmates, friends and family, because ITV wanted me to be the subject for one of the shows when I came back off tour. Everyone was lined up: John Stockley, Cliff Fleming and Derek Birchall, while layers like Allan Langer and Peter Sterling had been contacted, and everything was set. But my mum hadn't heard anything after that, so she rang the producer to see what was going on – and was stunned by the answer.

The producer told her: 'We've been told that Andrew no longer plays for Wigan, and that we should go for someone else instead.' He had the cheek to add that if I wanted to be a guest when they did Dean Bell, I'd be more than welcome. My answer was short and to the point, and its second word was 'off'. I don't know the strength of Maurice's part in that, and I don't think I ever will. But that's the way it was: I went to Leeds, I never got to go on *This Is Your Life*, and my mother has never forgiven or forgotten. Maybe I should have taken that as an indicator of how things would go at Leeds. If I had, I'd have avoided the worst time of my career, one which eventually saw me have to move to Salford before I grew so downhearted that I packed it up altogether.

Yet when Leeds initially came in for me, it seemed like an ideal opportunity at the time. I was only 31 and knew I was far from over the hill, while the £15,000 transfer fee was hardly going to break the bank for a club of that size. And it meant linking up with Doug Laughton once again, the man who had given me my big break in the early days with Widnes. Leeds had always been the great underachievers of rugby league, and the prospect of helping them back to the glory days was another huge incentive for me. On the face of it, they certainly looked to be heading in the right direction. Around that time they had also signed, or were on the point of signing, Ellery Hanley, Shaun Wane and Andy Goodway from Wigan, and my old pal Mike O'Neill from Widnes, while there were already top-flight players such as Garry Schofield at the club. But it didn't take long to shatter all my dreams.

The dressing-room may have been packed with high-quality players, but while they were struggling to put some silverware in the trophy cabinet, they'd have won every gold medal going if they were awarded for backbiting. There was a very definite Yorkshire-Lancashire split in the camp, and none of the after-hours socialising we had enjoyed during the halcyon days at Central Park. It didn't help that there seemed to be a huge rift between Ellery and Schoey, which petered through to everyone else. Ellery had been used to phenomenal success at Wigan, and desperately tried to turn it around when he arrived at Leeds. But I got the impression that Garry was quite happy to pick up the Man of the Match award week in, week out – but that wasn't doing a great deal to put something in the trophy cupboard. I felt sorry for Dougie, because he worked very hard to develop the youth side of things, and no one could complain about the facilities available to us. We had a great training set-up, and we wanted for nothing – but that didn't count for anything between 3.00 and 4.30 on a Sunday afternoon.

It didn't take too long for the travelling to start wearing me down, either. Don't forget, I had previously always played for clubs fairly close to home, so sitting in never-ending traffic jams on the M62 was something that was totally alien to me. And it wasn't an experience I was ever going to get used to. I used to drive over the Pennines with Andy, Mike and Shaun, and while we flew it on occasions, there were far too many times when it would take us up to four hours just to get to training. The Lancashire contingent used to meet up at Birch Services, and I lost count of the number of times when I was on the point of picking up the mobile, calling Doug and asking him if we could train nearer to home because we were stuck in traffic. And if you go into work depressed and aren't looking forward to it, then you are never going to do the job as well as you know you can.

I just wasn't enjoying my rugby, and that was something I had never felt before. In fact, during my time at Headingley – I was with Leeds for just over a season – I only had one half-decent game, against Castleford. It wasn't for the lack of trying on my part, despite what some people seemed to think. No one wanted the club to succeed more than me, and the fans were absolutely superb. They could see I was busting a gut, but just like that 1984 tour with Great Britain, I simply couldn't get my act together. They say that the harder you try, the worse it can get, and I think that was the case for me.

And as for team spirit: you couldn't have brightened it up if you'd brought in Ken Dodd, Bernard Manning and Chubby Brown. Not that anyone ever said anything to your face – it was all said behind your back. Ellery clearly didn't agree with a lot of the ideas that Doug had, but rarely discussed it with him, as you would have imagined he would. It was as though he wanted the coach's job himself, and I personally just could not work in that kind of atmosphere. Doug wanted to have meetings with the players to chew thing over but, quite honestly, I don't think he had any idea of all the backbiting that was going on.

Now we weren't all the best of mates at Wigan, but we knew that if our preparation was crap, then our performance on the field was likely to follow suit. We were professional enough to know how vital it was to gel, and we all pulled together in the same direction. At Leeds we were like a Red Arrows display team, all trying to do our own thing. At times after training, when we had difficulty picking something off the various choices provided on the lunch menu, I used to think back to the days when players would turn up for training after a day down the pit. We were there, with jacuzzis, massages, saunas, steam rooms . . . and a team that you wouldn't have backed to beat an egg. The old timers would have been turning in their graves at the thought of it.

There were too many Leeds players on easy street, and as far as I was concerned I couldn't get out of the place quick enough. I would like to stress again, though, that my feelings had nothing to do with how the fans were towards me. I had kicked them in the guts so many times with Wigan that I couldn't have complained if they had given me a hard time – but nothing could have been further from the truth. They were great to me, and they were great to Dawn.

In the end, Ellery played a significant part in my departure. He knew I wasn't playing well, and alerted Doug to the fact that Patrick Entat, the French scrum-half, was keen to come over to play in this country. He convinced the coach that Patrick would do a better job than me – and he did me a massive favour into the bargain! When Doug called me into his office and said that

Salford wanted me, it was patently obvious to both of us that I was on my way. Maybe in hindsight it would have been better for me if I had moved over to live in Yorkshire, but we can all be masters when we look back.

What summed it up for me was the way the players treated Andy Watson, the commercial manager at the club. He worked his guts out for Leeds, but was treated like crap by the lot of them. I used to talk to him at length, and I knew he was pulling his tripe out for them to make them a success. But he had no respect at all, and I was absolutely delighted for him when he picked up a job at Everton Football Club, and proved by his record there what a talent he was. He did a great job for the Toffees – not least by providing me with two tickets at the side of the Gwladys Street end whenever they played Manchester United! If everyone at Headingley had given the same amount of effort as Andy, then Leeds would have been nailed-on certs to pick up a trophy every season.

So when the chance came to join Salford, I was the happiest man in the world. They got me basically for free, but it had reached the stage when I would probably have paid a transfer fee myself just to escape from Headingley and get my sanity back. I also knew what I was going back to – to some extent, at least – because Albert White and the chairman John Wilkinson were big mates of mine. It was a little ironic that I had turned them down all those years earlier after the trial game against Barrow, and here I was now returning to the scene of where it almost all began. And the scene of where it was all to end – on both counts.

NINE

Donald, Mickey . . . and a Dead Cert

We not only had the most successful club side in rugby league history during my days at Wigan, we could also give anyone else in the game a good run when it came to having a laugh. And my big mate Joe Lydon was usually there or thereabouts when it came to the jokes.

At Christmas we'd have a big players' party, like every other side in the league. One particular year, ours happened to fall on the same night as a board meeting. This particular do was fancy dress: I'd gone as Mickey Mouse, and Joe as Donald Duck. Things were well under way, and we'd all had a few, when he and I decided to pop down and have a word with the directors. Picture the scene: a handful of middle-aged guys sitting around a table to discuss the running of rugby league's biggest club, when they were rudely interrupted by the door being flung open. You could have heard a pin drop when they were confronted by a 6ft duck and a 5ft mouse screaming at them: 'The trouble with this bloody club is that no one takes us seriously.'

While Joe was usually in the thick of the jokes, there was one occasion when his quick thinking saved the day for me. We were playing Widnes in a title decider, in front of 20,000 fans at Central Park and God knows how many more watching on Sky. I always seemed to have a run-in with Colin Morris whenever he refereed me, and this was no different. Early in the game he gave one decision which I really took exception to, so much so that I picked the ball up and threw it at him from 30 yards. It was winging straight for his head, when Joe appeared from nowhere and pulled off a save that Peter Schmeichel would have been proud of. He must have dived six feet to pluck the ball from the air inches from the ref's face. Off the field Colin and I actually got on fine, and it used to make me laugh when people thought we couldn't stand the sight of each other. There was never any problem with him personally in my view – I used to hate all refs, not just him.

Now no one in that Wigan side was particularly fond of losing – not that it was a habit we ever looked like getting into. But it got to the stage where we would be furious if we so much as let a try in. And on one occasion at Castleford, that led to an unforgettable moment. It was a horrible night, and they were really up for giving us a good seeing-to. But within 20 minutes we were out of sight, and we went on to win comfortably. Late in the game we conceded a try, and skipper Dean Bell was roasting us as we waited under the sticks for the conversion to be taken. Dean was really giving it to us, when someone on the terraces threw a snowball and it caught him full in the face. You've never seen so many players suddenly feeling the need to drop to their knees and fasten their bootlaces. At least it put a stop to the rollicking!

Great Britain tours had their moments as well – although when my big mate Roy Haggerty of St Helens was with the squad, they were quite often unintentional. One year we arrived in Australia to be greeted by all the dignitaries, and we had to go through the usual formal welcomes. Everyone was shaking hands and introducing themselves: I'm Andy Gregory fromWigan, I'm Martin Offiah from Wigan, I'm Mike Gregory from Warrington, and so on. Until it came to Roy's turn, when he uttered the immortal words: 'I'm Roy Haggerty . . . from Elephant Lane.'

One year Roy was with the squad for a game in France, and he'd been getting a bit of grief from his wife over what he might get up to while he was over there. He tried to reassure her that he would be spending most of his time in his hotel room watching TV. She said: 'Don't talk rubbish, you won't understand a word of it.' 'It's okay, love, I'll be fine,' said Roy. 'I'll take the portable.' And he couldn't understand why she wouldn't believe him!

Australia was the backdrop for a couple of other memorable episodes. During one close season Steve Hampson and I had a spell with Illawarra, Joe was at Easts, Ellery was with Wests and Shaun Edwards was playing for Balmain. Wigan had arranged a match against Warrington in Milwaukee, so we all had to fly to America for the game before heading back to Sydney. Hampo and Joe flew off after the match via Honolulu, while the rest of us were to go straight back – or so we planned. When we came to passport control, they wouldn't let us out of the country because we didn't have the necessary multiple-entry visas. So we spent three days in Chicago with virtually no money, while all our luggage was on its way back to Australia. Dawn was waiting for me in Sydney and didn't believe a word of it. I don't think any of our clubs did either.

We decided to pass a bit of time on the beach in Los Angeles, where Ellery and Shaun decided to go for a jog. I wasn't the most dedicated runner in the world at the best of times, so charging up and down the sand on a hot and humid day was a definite non-starter for me. I told them to go ahead while I stayed behind to look after what few belongings we had. Within ten seconds I was flat out, and if anyone had wanted to rob the gear, they could have taken me as well and I would have been none the wiser.

It was only a brief stay in LA before things were sorted out. But during that time we achieved the unique feat of managing to find a priest to chauffeur us around, who spent his time trying to sell us black market tickets for the Lakers, telling us where to get cheap booze, and how he could get us some hookers as well. And I don't mean bull-necked forwards to pack down in the scrum. Come to think of it, though, we never did get to see the Lakers . . .

That spell with Illawarra ended with me being taken for the biggest ride of my life. It had been a bit of a roller-coaster, to say the least, from the day we arrived. The club held a big reception in our honour, and got Hampo and I both on stage to welcome us officially. We shook hands with the chief executive, the coach, the captain . . . you name it. Now I have never been the biggest fan of that sort of thing, making speeches to all the fans through a microphone and suchlike. So I was glad when I'd said my piece, and moved aside to let Hampo do his bit. And I can honestly say I was only being friendly when I said to the main man's wife at the back of the stage: 'Hiya, love, when's the baby due?' You could have heard a pin drop as the mike picked it up, along with her reply : 'I'm not pregnant, I'm just fat.' I'm surprised they didn't send me home there and then.

Things could only pick up, and they duly did, when Hampo

and I helped Illawarra to the Panasonic Cup final for the first time in their history. So by the time we were due to go back to England we were big heroes there – especially in the Harp Hotel, where we spent countless nights having a giggle and a drink. But on the final night, the laugh was most definitely on yours truly, as they stitched me up good and proper.

They threw a big party in our honour, and there must have been 300 people at it. We had a big barbecue, the drink was flowing, and we didn't even have to leave the place to place a bet, because all the Aussie bars had an in-house TAB – similar to the Tote over here – where we could have a flutter. Now we had lost the Panasonic Cup to Brisbane, but I'd won the Man of the Match award, which was $10,000 worth of electrical gear. There was no way I could get that back to England, so I had sold it back to the club, not thinking of how I would be able to take that much money out of the country. Even so, it meant I had a nice few quid in my pocket for the leaving party, which was going full steam ahead.

We were all having a pint and a punt, when one bloke said to me: 'There's a big tip running in the 3.50 at Brisbane. We can't get it on the screen [which was true] but there will be commentary.' Winter Splash was the horse's name, and everyone was raving about it, so I stuck all my money on it. A couple of minutes before the off I was starting to wonder if I'd done the right thing, but everyone else was on it, and it was too late to back out. Over they went to Brisbane for the commentary, and after a slow start Winter Splash finished like a train and got up on the line to win.

I've never moved so fast in my life: I charged around the pub punching the air and buying drinks. It was the biggest round I've ever bought – one for every person in there. When I calmed down enough to ask the starting price, I was staggered to find it had gone off at 33–1. Never mind smuggling $10,000 out of the country, I spent the next half hour thinking of ways to get all this back home. I was going to give some to Dawn to hide, put some in Lauren's pram – you name it, I came up with it.

After another hour or so, an old chap came up with a photo of a horse and said: 'It's a bloody good 'un, that Winter Splash.' I agreed and bought him a drink. 'Mind you,' he added, 'it bloody should be – it won that same race 15 years ago.'

The place fell about as the penny dropped. Every single person in the pub was in on the act. They'd set up the Pommie good style. I just put my head in my hands and said: 'You bunch of so-and-sos – how could you do this to me?' One bloke strolled up, put his hand on my shoulder and replied: 'For three and a half months you've done nothing but take the mickey out of us. Don't tell us you expected us to let you go home without getting our own back.' At least the swine had the decency to return my stake. But I didn't buy them any more drinks.

TEN

The British Bulldog

I have never been particularly fond of France, from the moment I made my Great Britain début against that country in 1981. My first appearance came at the Boulevard, in Hull, and we celebrated with a 37–0 victory. In the return match in Marseilles, the main thing that sticks in the memory was all the trouble. There always seemed to be at least one incident when we played the French, and this was no different.

To me, trips across the Channel to play France meant the misery of a couple of nights living off ham and French stick. People go on about the marvellous culture of the place, and the fabulous cuisine, but for me you can keep it. And I wasn't the only one who had that opinion. So much so that, on certain occasions when I had a niggling injury, I even pulled out of the Great Britain squad to play there. In hindsight that is something I regret, because the opportunity to represent your country against anyone should be something to savour. But that was how strongly I dislike the French.

One of the toughest players I ever came up against, or stood shoulder to shoulder with, was a guy called Alan Rathbone. The second time I visited France, in 1983, the match was right up his street. There had been trouble all afternoon, and we were all surprised when, about two minutes from time, a game of rugby broke out! There was one particular incident, though, which was one of the worst I've witnessed. The French had collapsed a scrum, and the ball was stuck between someone's legs. Alan shouted to me to get rid of it quickly, but there was no way I was sticking my hands or head anywhere near it. When a slight gap appeared Alan, being the lad he was, put his head in to clear the ball – and as soon as he did, a French forward booted him full in the face. It all kicked off from there, and even carried on as we headed down the tunnel after the final hooter. Let's just say that Alan more than got his own back. There weren't too many who came out of it on top when they took him on.

However little I thought of France, at least it had given me a first taste of international football. Now I was after a crack at the biggie – the mighty Australians. That chance came in 1982, and was the first of six Ashes series I played against them. I had been overlooked for the first two Tests, when Great Britain were thumped by a side they were already referring to as 'The Invincibles', but I got my chance in the last game. There were a few new faces in that side – people such as Brian Noble, Mike O'Neill, Mick Crane and Lee Crooks all came in, although everyone still expected them to give us another hiding. But for an hour we more than held our own, and we were even thinking in terms of the unlikeliest win ever when Kangaroo back-rower Wayne Pearce made a break from halfway that opened the floodgates. The Aussies finished that tour unbeaten, but that was of no concern to me – I'd had a taste of playing the best, and I wanted more of it.

My chance came in 1984 when Great Britain travelled to Australia. I went over as the best half-back in the country, only to suffer a complete nightmare Down Under. In fact, I went from being the nation's top scrum-half to third choice behind Neil Holding and Ray Ashton in the space of a few short weeks. I was so poor on that trip that if every half-back in the game had gone over, I reckon I'd still have been bottom of the pile. It wasn't deliberate, and it wasn't through lack of effort: it was just one of those phases when nothing comes off. The only memorable thing for me was playing at Sydney Cricket Ground against Norths. I'd seen my big mate, Neil Fairbrother, playing cricket there and I always wanted to do the same. The highlight of the whole trip was walking out on to that field to play for Great Britain – not that it stopped me having another shocker. I had a terrible time from day one, and was dropped for all three Australian Tests. To make matters worse, I rang home one day to discover that my mum had been in a car crash – it was the lowest single point of my playing career.

I felt the Great Britain management let us down throughout the trip, which didn't help matters. When we were in Sydney we stayed at the Sheraton Wentworth Hotel, which was basically too posh for us. We wanted a hotel where we could lounge about in our kit, but this lot didn't even like us walking through the foyer in it after training. Some of the lads wanted to hang their washing out over the balcony, but as soon as they did there would be a knock on the door from the porter to complain about it. You can imagine what they thought when Mike Nicholas, the former Warrington and Wales forward who is one of my biggest mates, turned up in a battered old hillbilly van. We thought Jed Clampett had joined the official supporters' pary! Although we laughed, that van got him all over Australia to follow us, and it was typical of Nico.

We had a meeting with Dick Gemmell, the tour manager, and put it to him that we would be better off staying somewhere else. We were all trying to save money, and we wanted as much as possible left at the end of the tour to share between us, because everyone had bills and mortgages to pay back home. But Dick was staying in a top suite that must have cost a fortune, there was nothing cheap on the menu, and as far as we were concerned it was frittering money away. But nothing came of the meeting, and team spirit slumped even lower.

One guy I did feel sorry for was Rod McKenzie, our fitness trainer. He came from Carnegie College in Leeds and was more used to working with international athletes. What he couldn't accept was that it was a totally different ball game training rugby players. It was no good for us to run around Sydney the day after a game – we needed 24 hours to let the bangs ease up a bit. We were getting bashed all over the place – certainly a lot more than 200-metre runners ever did!

Frank Myler, the coach, tried his best, but it made me laugh when he used to write his team selection on the back of a matchbox during the training sessions. The way I was playing, we'd have had more chance with Captain Webb at half-back than me. Frank suffered a massive blow when Tony Myler – possibly the most gifted stand-off I ever played with – was dogged by injuries on the tour. Tony wasn't right when we arrived, but the management were giving him cortisone jabs just to get him to training, never mind the matches. Ultimately, I believe that knocked years off his career.

Things picked up a bit – personally, at least – on the New Zealand leg. We still lost the series against the Kiwis 3–0, but I was our Man of the Match in two of the games, and had to defuse a potentially very embarrassing situation after the second Test. Everyone had been bagging us as a useless bunch of Poms, so Frank wanted us to boycott the post-match ceremony. In my view, that would have led to more criticism and being labelled bad losers. So we talked him into going along, and an awkward incident was averted.

From there it was on to Papua New Guinea, and although we actually won the Test there, it was a still a pretty miserable squad which arrived back in England – and I walked straight into those problems with Widnes. I've already explained how they were sorted out with my move to Warrington. But although I was playing some brilliant rugby at Wilderspool, the new Great Britain coach, Maurice Bamford, still left me out in the cold for the best part of 18 months. To this day I don't know why. Eventually Bamford quit the post, Malcolm Reilly took over, and my international career took off once more.

In 1988 we were off Down Under for another Ashes series – and a tour that was memorable for (mainly) the right reasons. There were some great characters on that trip, people like Mike Gregory, myself, Phil Ford and Andy Platt. Most nights we ended up having to buy Fordy a pair of sunglasses, because his eyes went all bloodshot after a couple of pints, and we needed to sneak past Mal on the way back to our rooms.

The Aussies were still pretty much untouchable at the time, but at half-time in the first Test we were winning 6–0. Yet instead of sitting down and taking stock in the dressing-room, we all became Grade One coaches and started bellowing about what we were going to do in the second half. I think that's where we lost it, because Australia came back to win 17–6. At least we emerged with a lot of credit and our pride intact. And, of course, there were still two Test matches left.

In the build-up to the first Test we had played at Newcastle, and I was Man of the Match again. Afterwards I did all the usual interviews with the press, so they all knew I had come out of it without any injury problems. It took some explaining, then, when I emerged next morning as one of our walking wounded. I had been out to celebrate the win with the usual suspects – Platty, Mike Greg, Fordy and Lee Crooks. As I was coming out of the lift in the hotel at about 2 a.m., Mike decided to throw an ironing board at me. He caught me full on the hand with such force that the bone came through the skin of my finger. We knocked up Forbes Mackenzie, the tour doctor, at about 3 a.m. and explained to him that I had trapped it in the lift doors. The next day I couldn't take part in any of the ball work at training, so we had to stick to the same story for all the press lads.

We went into the second Test with huge hopes of a victory. Twenty minutes in that was all out of the window, as the Aussies rattled up a ten-point lead. The Lang Park crowd really gave us the bird, and by half-time the game was effectively over. When they scored again with about ten minutes to go, and we were under the sticks waiting for another conversion, I asked the other lads, 'Have you got any pride? We are a disgrace and they're all laughing at us.' Second row Roy Powell, as nice a guy as you could wish to meet despite his fearsome frame, piped up in his high-pitched voice, 'Let's get motivated – give it a go.' Maybe it was because it was so unexpected for Roy to get worked up, but something sent me over the edge. Whatever the reason, a few minutes later Andrew Ettingshausen took the ball, and I caught him with a pearler of a high shot. That was my game over: sin-binned, although it might as well have been a red card as there was hardly any time left.

If we had all believed our own publicity a little too much beforehand, we certainly didn't get much positive stuff afterwards. For an entire week Peter Moore, the main man at Canterbury Bankstown, really slagged me off, and I remember the *Sydney Morning Herald* in particular coming out with some very nasty stuff. I knew I hadn't played well, and I had lost my head at the end, but I didn't think I deserved the amount of flak they were throwing in my direction.

By the day of the third Test, we had been written off as such a bunch of losers that the attendance was atrocious. On the face of it, you wouldn't have given us much chance of proving them wrong, either. Players were dropping like flies, and I think we only had one fit substitute going into the game. But the old British Lion is never more dangerous than when it's wounded, and so it turned out. Fordy stepped through for a marvellous try, Henderson Gill strolled past full-back Garry Jack for another, and Mike Gregory capped it all by going 70 yards after I put him through a gap. Ten points clear at half-time, we wound up winning 26–12.

After everything that had been said and written about us, it was a great way to bounce back – even if we had lost the series. To cap it all, Peter Moore had to present me with my award as Man of the Match, and made this speech about what a great player I was. I hope that there will be plenty of kids who will read this book, so I won't tell you exactly what my reply was. Suffice to say, it was a lot stronger than, 'Thanks, Pete, much appreciated.' I ended that night sitting in Paul and David Hulme's room, eating chips out of a champagne bucket. It was great to see their dad, Matty, enjoying the moment because he had been everywhere supporting his lads. Dawn was out there too, as well as my big mate Mike Nicholas and a few others – it was magnificent for them as much as us.

Even Malcolm let his hair down the next day when we flew across the Tasman to New Zealand – and into another storm. We played the Kiwis in a World Cup-ranked game to decide who faced the Aussies in the final – and to this day I think someone had already decided it wouldn't be Great Britain. New Zealand knocked Ellery Hanley out of the game, we had a perfectly good try disallowed and they went on to beat us by two points. Perhaps the organisers were after a Southern Hemisphere local derby in the final, because that's what they got. I have always tried to be dignified in defeat, but I must admit I found it very difficult that day, because we all felt as though we had been cheated out of it.

Still, there would always be another tour and another Ashes series. But although I didn't know it then, the next time I would travel to Australia with Great Britain would be the biggest disappointment of all.

ELEVEN

A Tour Too Far

After the 1988 tour I stayed Down Under to play for the Rest of the World against the Aussies as part of their bicentennial. I think they were treating it as little more than a showpiece match, but as far as I was concerned it was a chance to show that I was up to the standards of local heroes such as Peter Sterling, Allan Langer and Wally Lewis. So maybe Steve Roach, the Kangaroo prop and a big pal of mine, shouldn't have been too surprised when I blacked his eye in a tackle. Old Blocker wasn't too chuffed after the game when his wife asked him what had happened. He nodded at me and said, 'Just ask my Pommie pal – he's the one who gave me a sly dig.' Yet that's the way it was with me, and it was certainly no reflection of what I thought of Australia. If I had something against either the country or the Aussies, I wouldn't have been there ten times.

When I got home everyone was talking about how Great Britain had closed the gap on Australia, even though I still felt we had some way to go. But at least we had done enough in that last Test to know that we could give them a beating, and we went into the next series against them in 1990 full of confidence. Everything about the build-up to the first Test at Wembley had been perfect. The side was packed with Wigan players who were on the top of their game, and the Rugby Football League pulled off a master-stroke by blasting 'Land of Hope and Glory' around the stadium as we walked out of the tunnel. That made us all feel ten feet tall – that's a hell of an increase for someone like me – and you could see the Aussies wondering what on earth they were stepping into.

It certainly had the desired effect because we turned them over, and suddenly we were within sight of a first Ashes triumph since 1970. The gap between the two countries was definitely smaller than I could ever remember, and there were just as many tipping us to win the second Test at Old Trafford as them. It was all square going into the last minute there, when Kangaroo half-back Ricky Stuart threw a dummy, Lee Jackson took it, and he went the length of the field before setting up Mal Meninga for the match-winner. So that was that – the series was level 1-1, and the Aussies were out of jail and suddenly in the ascendancy going into the decider at Elland Road.

I don't know why, but for some reason I had a real pessimistic feeling about that game. As we got on to the coach to go to the ground, I still remember thinking that we had had our chance, and the Aussies were going to win the series. It was the only time in my life that I went into any game, as a player or a coach, thinking that we weren't going to win – and so it proved. If there's one thing Australians do better than anyone, it's defend, and that's exactly how they beat us that day. They snuffed out every option we tried, they took the chances they created, and they won quite easily in the end. After all the euphoria following the Wembley win, that was a bitter, bitter disappointment to us all.

At least the next time I was in Australia I came away as a winner, albeit at club level. Yet if Maurice Lindsay had had his way, I wouldn't have gone at all. Wigan were invited to take part in the 1992 Sydney Sevens, but before we left Maurice told coach John Monie that I wasn't suited to it and shouldn't go. To his eternal credit John replied, 'Can you imagine what Greg will be like when we get back – if he doesn't go, then neither do I.' Needless to say, I was in the squad that flew out of Manchester.

Our wingers Martin Offiah and David Myers had a bet between themselves as to who would score the most tries in the tournament. It soon became obvious who would win. In our first game against Cronulla, Dave made a break and a prop-forward caught him! Did he get any stick from the lads for that? What do you think? The next morning I was awoken at about 6 a.m. by a noise in the hotel corridor. It started as a slow walk, developed into a jog and ended with a thunderous sprint. After about ten minutes, I stuck my head out of the door and saw Dave charging up and down. He looked at me and said, 'I'm not bloody getting caught again – I'm building my speed up, Greg.'

He obviously didn't go about it the right way, because he ended the tournament without a try, Martin was top scorer with ten, and even I managed to cross against Penrith – which was one more than Dave got.

We were all there to win, but halfway through a long domestic season no one was too gutted to lose one of the early games and be knocked out. Or at least we thought we were. Everyone was sitting around enjoying a chat and a laugh at the Sydney Football Stadium, when Maurice came running up. We had actually qualified for the latter stages of the competition, and went out the next day to beat Manly and then Brisbane in the final, courtesy of a hat-trick from Offiah.

Martin's performances on the field did more than anything to win the trophy, but a lot of the credit for it should go to Bob Lanigan, our conditioner. When he came to Wigan he brought a new dimension to training, and he is probably as responsible as anyone for the way in which outlooks have improved so much over recent years. Not that we always agreed with his methods. When we arrived in Sydney for the Sevens, Bob had us out on the training field just a couple of hours into our stay. You can imagine our delight when he told us that we were going to do 32 short sprints to 'blow away a few cobwebs'. Everyone looked at each other in horror, and Gene Miles piped up from the back: 'Jeez, Bob – can we not just do one long one?'

But if that was a memorable trip to Australia my next one with Great Britain on the 1992 tour was instantly forgettable. If only I could. I had actually retired from international football after the 1990 series, but Malcolm and Maurice had collared me after I'd had a stormer for Wigan in one game at Hull KR. Maybe my guard was down a little, maybe it was pride; but when they asked me to have one more crack at the Aussies I eventually agreed. Big mistake!

It all started well enough as I put Platty in for two tries against Canberra Raiders, although I ended the game on the bench and in pain with a pulled muscle in my groin. After that it was uphill all the way. I shouldn't really have been in the side for the first Test, but after the way I had played against the Raiders the management were desperate for me to play, and I bowed to the pressure. I knew I was very doubtful to last the full 80 minutes as we came out of the tunnel at the Sydney Football Stadium, because there were times when I couldn't even run properly. Things went from bad to worse when I caught stand-off Peter Jackson with a high tackle early in the game and was sin-binned.

I had only been back on the field for a few minutes when one of the worst – and certainly one of the most mystifying –

incidents took place. Prop-forward Ian Lucas went into a tackle with Paul Harragon and ended up spark out. I was only about three yards away from the collision – only Ian was closer – and to this day I couldn't tell you what happened. I don't know if Harragon caught him with his elbow, his fist, his head, or just put in a huge tackle. My first instinct was to give him a belt, but after being sin-binned already, that would have been the end of my game, and for once my head ruled my heart. We went on to lose the game, but that was nothing compared to the feeling of walking off the pitch and seeing Ian, a Wigan team-mate of mine, lying on a stretcher with an oxygen mask and all sorts of wires attached to him. That definitely put the match into perspective.

To make matters worse, I was the one who got pulled out for a random drugs test after the match. Not that it was a problem. Never mind not using drugs, I haven't even ever had a cigarette. Just like I've never sprinted 60 yards to congratulate someone on scoring a try. To be honest, I have never seen the point in charging upfield to shake hands with someone who has got to come back to you anyway. Maybe that's why I never felt the need to take a drink on the field. These days there are blokes running on with water bottles even before the kick-off. I didn't realise you could burn off so much energy just walking out of the tunnel!

Back on the tour, our next game was against a New South Wales country side up in Parkes. I was already taking tablets and having daily treatment just to get onto the training field, but the jibes were starting to emerge. I knew I wasn't playing up to my own standards, but I also knew why. More to the point, so did the British management who had talked me into going in the first place. But that didn't stop Dave Graham, the tour doctor, coming to my room in Parkes and telling me that I had to declare myself fit to play. I told him I wasn't, and he replied that if that was the case, then I would have to go home. Once again I decided to give it a go, but by this time I was totally disillusioned with the management. They had twisted my arm to come out of international retirement, and as soon as it went wrong I was thrown into the corner like a rag doll.

To be fair, by that stage I think they were just as sick of me as I was of them. They knew I wasn't playing well, and it was patently obvious to everyone that I just wasn't enjoying it. Having said that, I had still given my all in every match, even though I had effectively gone into the first Test on one leg.

It all came to a head when I played what turned out to be my final game of international rugby league in Parkes. I gouged and bit a guy out of sheer frustration – actually, I did it to a few of them. It's not something I am proud of, but it shows you exactly how low I was feeling. Naturally there was a big outcry about it all, and Frank Fish, the home team's manager, caused a real stink by labelling the Brits 'biters'. The management sprang to our defence, and the whole thing eventually blew over, but I think they knew what I had done. By then things were so bad that Malcolm and I weren't even really speaking to each other.

We had a meeting, and it was decided that it would be better for everyone if I took no further part in the tour. To be honest, by that stage I wasn't particularly bothered about it – in fact, if anything, I was pleased – even though I knew that my international career had come to a halt. I flew home with Ian Lucas, who was still in a bad way, and totally subdued on the way back. He was still suffering from dizzy spells; he wasn't at all well and was never really the same again. I guess that tended to put my own problems into perspective, because at least I still had my health.

I watched the second Test, Great Britain's historic 33–10 win in Melbourne, in the studio where I was working for Sky. Plenty of people have asked me since if I had mixed feelings as I saw the lads pull off that famous victory. But I can honestly say that there wasn't a happier Brit than me when they did it. I know there are certain players who don't like to see their team-mates do well if they aren't playing, but there was none of that with me. It never crossed my mind that I could have been in the team that ran up that record win. As far as I was concerned, we could win 1–0 or 50–0 – a victory was a victory in my book. It didn't matter what the scoreboard said at the end of the game, so long as my team had more points than the other. In fact, I have never taken any notice of records throughout my career, even though I was obviously very honoured to pick up things like the two Lance Todd Trophies. All the glory comes from performances on the field, and as far as I was concerned the fact that the Lions had won was good enough for me.

The only regret I had about the whole tour was that I had gone on it in the first place. I really should have listened to my head and stuck to my guns. That is possibly the biggest problem I have had throughout my life – I have always helped others when I should have been putting Andy Gregory first. It's a lesson that took a long time to sink in.

TWELVE

Going Back to my Roots

Things had gone from bad to worse after that 1992 tour. Not only had my time at Wigan come to an unpleasant end, I had stepped out of the frying pan and into the fire with that ill-fated move to Leeds. So there couldn't have been a brighter light at the end of the tunnel than when Salford effectively saved my career by signing me.

I'm not being over dramatic when I say that, if things had gone on for much longer at Headingley, then I honestly think I would have packed up everything. There was also more than a hint of returning to my roots by joining Salford. Don't forget, Albert White was the man who had been responsible for that infamous first taste of senior action, when I had torn Barrow apart as an unnamed trialist. Albert is, and always will be, a big mate of mine. And I have got plenty of time for chairman John Wilkinson, too.

I didn't actually play that many games at the Willows, but it was a real relief to be back in a changing room that had a good team spirit. I know Garry Jack, the Salford coach, had big doubts about signing me, but that was possibly because there was a bit of a history between us from our clashes at international level. Garry had been full-back for Australia against Great Britain on numerous occasions, and there had been a few times when I had run-ins with him. He had bagged me in games more than once, I had not been slow to give it back, and we had also had the odd dig in the tackle. So he was one man I didn't get on particularly well with at Salford, although there were no problems with anyone else. I also think Garry had a few suspicions about my reasons for signing; perhaps he was frightened that I had designs on his job.

It's a little ironic that I did end up succeeding him as coach – and if I am honest I must admit that to some extent I did go to Salford with half an eye on the coaching role. But I never signed with the intention of getting Garry Jack sacked. For the time being, I was more than happy simply giving my all as a player. But, naturally enough for Andy Gregory, there had to be the odd twist in the tale – and it came in a game that led to the most embarrassing incident of my entire career.

One thing I had always managed to do was keep my home life and my playing life separate. By that, I mean that whatever went on away from the field never affected me on it. Apart from this particularly dreadful occasion – and of all the games, it had to be the one when Lauren was Salford's mascot. We were playing Bradford in a televised Sky game on a Friday night, and I'd had a bad time of it in the scrapyard and at home. To make matters worse, the weather was awful, although that hardly excused my actions. Bradford got off to a good start, and we were up against it from the first few minutes. I could see Lauren standing at the side of the tunnel shivering in the freezing cold conditions, and that was getting to me as well.

They had just scored their second try to go 10–0 up. I was feeling totally dejected as we waited for the conversion, thinking, 'What the heck am I doing here?' For some reason their big prop Paul Grayshon decided to tell me, 'I'm really going to give it to you, Gregory.' That was a big mistake, the way I was feeling, even though I had never had any run-ins with him in the past. Within 30 seconds of passing on that kind warning he was being carried off, and I was on my way down the tunnel after being sent off. Straight from the kick-off he caught the ball and drove it in – only for me to flatten him with a ferocious high shot. When it happened, John Wilkinson turned to Albert and said, 'I don't think Andy actually caught him there.' He just looked back at Wilkie and said, 'He caught him all right, chairman, you mark my words.'

Albert came down to see me in the dressing-room and said, 'You'll cop a few games for that, won't you?' To be honest, at that stage I couldn't have cared less. After a while I threw my kit off and headed for the showers, and was standing there considering the impact of what I had done when the Salford kitman – a bloke we all affectionately called Taz – came strolling through. Taz was a huge Swinton fan, a cracking fellow, and about my size. That was quite fortunate because – as his nickname implies – if he'd been 6ft 6in. tall he would probably have killed someone. As I said, he was a smashing bloke, but when he lost his rag he was the nastiest piece of work you've ever seen in your life.

By this time Grayshon had obviously regathered his senses, because he came storming up looking for revenge. Don't forget that Lauren was the mascot and, unknown to me, she was standing outside the changing-rooms waiting for her dad. When Grayshon appeared, Taz – all 4ft 4in. of him – jumped between us before anything kicked off. Grayshon told me what he planned to do to me, and I just looked back and said, 'I've done you once, and it will be no trouble to do you again, you big fat so-and-so.' With a few expletives thrown in for good measure. Grayshon turned around and went back to the Bradford dressing-room, where I could hear him continuing to shout about what he was going to do to Gregory, so I gave him another dose of the verbals. At which point Lauren walked through the door and said, 'Dad, I'm sure I have just heard you swearing at that man.'

Never mind the sending-off, never mind the fact it was televised – that one moment made me feel worse than you could possibly imagine. What a great example I had set, and on her big night as well. She had been looking forward to it for ages, and of all the people to ruin it, it had been her dad.

Up to that point, anything that had gone on at home, work or wherever had been cast aside while I was out on the field. But for some reason I had taken all my domestic frustrations and pent-up aggression into the game, and it had come out in the worst possible way. I certainly didn't keep the video of that match. To be honest, I don't think I have ever watched a tape of a game I have played in all the way through.

When I had the house in Grappenhall, you could have walked in and never known that a professional sportsman lived there. There was nothing around to give a clue – Lloyd Grossman would have had a devil of a job presenting that one on *Through the Keyhole*. It was the same story with my medals, which I used to keep in a Kwiksave bag – although I have since put them in a safety deposit box for Lauren.

Fame just came to me, I didn't go looking for it. Even now if I walk down the street, there is always someone wanting to chat. But that's just the way it is, and you have to accept it – although by then I was hardly the best company, because I just wasn't enjoying my rugby.

pint size

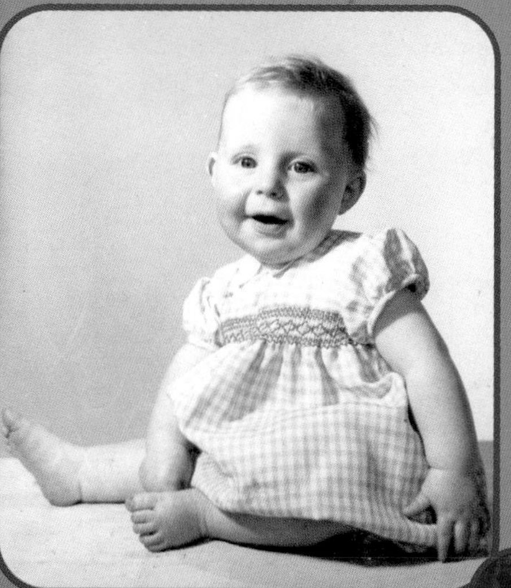

Butter wouldn't melt . . . do you get the impression Mum wanted a girl?

Prize guy . . . getting my first-ever award – for a children's running race – off Uncle Ron at Butlin's, 1966

The great de-bait! Going fishing with Bryn (left) and Neil

RIGHT: More tea vicar? Maybe now people will believe I was a choirboy, with St Mary's Church of England in Lower Ince

BELOW: The Dean Machine . . . Deanery MS Football Team, featuring my big mates Paul Spencer (back row, left), Trevor Stockley (back row, fourth right) and Tracey Grundy (front row, second right). I'm in the front row, second from the right

My hairo! Amateur days, amateur haircut, starring for Great Britain BARLA

Top Dog . . . BARLA Player of the Year in 1979

Shaw Fire Winner. Glyn Shaw gives me a lift after Widnes beat Hull KR in 1981

LEFT: First of many – lifting the Challenge Cup in 1981

BELOW: Cuppa Glee. My favourite sporting photo, with Grandad Harold after Widnes' 1981 Wembley triumph

By hooker, by crook . . . New Year's Eve fancy dress party, 1980

Oh baby . . . with Dawn at Lauren's christening

Muddy Hell . . . I have to admit there were days when you wondered if it was really worth it

Dad's the way to do it . . . celebrating Wigan's 1990 Challenge Cup win with Lauren

Famous last words. With Mavis (left), Mum and Bryn at Wigan's Hall of Fame dinner. Two days later I was out of a job

Four musketeers . . . with Cliff Fleming (left), Derek Birchall (centre) and Neil Hilton at the Hall of Fame dinner

Things finally came to a head one night in 1995 when I was speaking at a sportsman's dinner for former players. All the old Great Britain faces from years ago were there, and if anything convinced me that the time had finally come to get a couple of six-inch nails and hang up the old boots, it was that evening. I had always said that I wanted a life after rugby, and I didn't want to be one of those guys who could only get about with the aid of a walking stick. Of course I had picked up a few bangs throughout my career, but by and large I had been fairly lucky with injuries, apart from those couple of broken bones in quick succession in the early days at Widnes. But that night I lost count of the number of stories I heard from players who were struggling with various problems – some of them were waiting for new knees, others were due to have plastic hips or shoulders.

If I had a pound for every time someone told me that they couldn't get about like they used to do, I'd have retired to the South of France about ten years ago. I didn't want to end up in a wheelchair – I wanted to enjoy life after I had stopped playing. I had it all mapped out: play the odd game of five-a-side, go to the Daresbury Park Hotel to relax with mates like Steve Reed and Richard Gray, do a bit of training, have a laugh with good pals like Mike Nicholas. One of my big mates, the late Mike Slater, had got me into golf a few years earlier, and I fancied a few rounds. Maybe I knocked a couple of years off my career by deciding to quit when I did, but I have no regrets about it. And by then I was also coaching, so it wasn't as though I was turning my back on the game for good.

I had got the Salford job in March 1995, after an awful string of results finally spelled the end for Garry Jack. The crowd had turned against him, and as soon as that happens you have a heck of a job to win them back. There was quite a bit of ill feeling at the time, because Garry reckoned I had gone behind his back to get him the bullet and take his job – but that wasn't the case at all. I had spoken to people about where I thought we were going wrong, and what I saw as the problem, but that was only because I wanted the best for the club – my own ambitions didn't come into it. If that made Garry call me all the names under the sun, then fair enough, but it was pathetic.

One particular incident proved how petty the whole thing was, and how childish Jack could be. It was around the time when the powers-that-be were deciding which teams would get the nod to go into Super League. I had just discovered that Salford hadn't made it, and obviously we were all very down about it. My mobile phone rang, I answered it, and an Australian voice said, 'I'm f***ing made up that you've not got in.' I rang the number back, and it was a public telephone in the departure lounge at Manchester Airport. Jack had waited in the country long enough to hear the decision, and that was his final act before heading back to Australia. If anything, that made me even more determined to take Salford all the way back to the top – so thanks for that extra little incentive, Garry. No doubt you'll be glad to see that we made it in the end. When I took over as Salford coach it was like being back at Leeds all over again, the team spirit was so low. The camp had been more or less split in half – some had wanted Garry in charge, others wanted me – and the club had been forced to act. But it was definitely their choice, I can say that with hand on heart: I certainly didn't go storming into the boardroom saying the club is falling apart, you've got to get rid of the coach. They had asked me, as one of the senior players, what the mood was like in the dressing-room, and I told them that the spirit was very poor. That wasn't telling tales out of school, it was simply a case of being truthful, and anyone who was there at the time will back me up on that. The board then told me that they couldn't sack Garry, purely and simply because they couldn't afford to. But that argument didn't really hold up, because even if they had given him the bullet when the problems first started, they wouldn't then have had to pay him until the end of the season. No one likes sacking people, or seeing people on the receiving end of it, but it is a fact of life.

The club I took over was a shambles. By the time they turned to me, the players were largely doing what they wanted to, there was no discipline, people were turning up late for training – in a nutshell, it just wasn't a professional outfit. I didn't give them any big speeches about what we were going to do, or march in and start thumping my chest. I just told them that we all had to pull together, or we would sink even lower and never get into Super League. I reassured them that I wasn't about to go out and buy a whole new team. But by the same token, they had to prove to me that they were proud to wear the Salford shirt; we certainly weren't in a position where we could afford to carry any passengers. And to be fair to the players, they all responded magnificently – but not before we got another couple of kicks in the teeth along the way.

THIRTEEN

Room at the Top

My first full season in charge at the Willows was the last winter campaign which preceded the inaugural Super League summer. And it really rankled that it kicked off with Salford languishing in the lower division. I don't mean to run down the teams we were up against, but after spending my whole career winning trophies and playing at big stadiums, it was soul-destroying at times. If ever the point needed ramming home, it came in one of our first games that season – a Tuesday night up at Whitehaven, in front of little more than two men and a dog, with more atmosphere on the moon. I think that's when it really came home to roost that we desperately needed to get into Super League, or we would just fade away into obscurity.

But it wasn't going to be a case of simply turning up, going through the motions for a few months, and then taking our rightful place alongside Wigan, St Helens, Bradford and the rest.

We weren't even the bookmakers' favourites to win the First Division: that honour went to Keighley, who were going for broke by spending a lot of money on players. But titles aren't won in the offices of William Hill or Ladbrokes, and we went on to top the league – only to suffer the heartbreak of being denied a place in Super League because the powers-that-be decided not to offer promotion that season.

We knew we had to go out again in the first summer season and do it all again. Only this time it was going to be twice as hard, because we were the team that everyone wanted to beat. I firmly believe that the game's big chiefs really aren't that keen on teams like Salford being up there – and that stands to this day. I even had a meeting with John Wilkinson and told him that the easiest way to make sure we were promoted was to change our name to Manchester. There was all this talk about Super League wanting big-city teams, and we could have shot into that bracket purely by altering our title.

Of course it was a massive blow when we had missed out on Super League initially, and an even bigger disappointment when we didn't get in after winning the First Division. But we weren't going to get there by moping around and feeling sorry for ourselves. Once again, the players rolled up their sleeves and battled their way to the top. We had some cracking games along the way with Keighley, our biggest rivals for promotion, but there were a few nagging doubts at the back of my mind. The closer we got to the end of the season, the more it began to gnaw away at me that they would find a reason to keep us out. Assuming we won the title, of course.

To be honest, I had already made the decision that if we were denied a place in Super League for a second time, I would probably call it a day. As I said, I had played in the biggest stadiums in the world, Wembley had become a second home, I had won virtually every honour going, and I wanted to be back on the big stage. I certainly had no intention of ending my rugby league days in the wilderness, and there was a danger that if we didn't make it this time, we might not make it at all. I had found it hard to adjust to spending every other Sunday at places like Rochdale – with all due respect to them. The Salford changing-rooms are hardly like those at the Sydney Football Stadium, but compared to some of the places we travelled to, they were luxurious. I can't really pick out any one of the away grounds as being the worst, because they all seemed as bad as each other. I'm not knocking them, but it was a real culture shock.

I remember going to one of the Yorkshire clubs – I think it was Dewsbury or Doncaster – and their chairman asking Albert White if he thought it would be possible for me to go into their boardroom and have a chat with the directors. There was nothing sinister going on; they just wanted me to speak to them on a social basis, as someone who had played at the top level for years. Albert gave him an old-fashioned look and said, 'There's no chance of that – we can't even get him in ours.' It wasn't that I had anything against chairmen or directors, but it just wasn't my scene. It never has been. After a match, all I ever wanted to do was go in the players' bar and wind down with a couple of quiet pints with my friends. I certainly didn't need to sit down and analyse every aspect of the game.

By now I had fully adjusted to life purely as a coach, rather than combining it with playing, but my will to win was as high as ever. So no one was more delighted than me when we finished the 1996 season on top of the pile once more, and capped it all by going to on Old Trafford and winning the Divisional Premiership as well. After we'd done all that, there was no way they could deny us our rightful place in Super League.

I knew that if we were to survive and be successful in the higher division, we would have to do some serious team strengthening – and that meant making some very tough decisions. The hardest one of the lot was telling my old Wigan team-mate, Steve Hampson, that his services were no longer required. I had been pondering it for a while, but what finally made my mind up was one incident late in the season in a game against Keighley. Phil Cantillon, their hooker, made a break from just inside his own half and strolled around Hampo before scoring in the corner. Everyone was saying what a great try it was, but I saw it differently. I know Phil is one of the quicker forwards around, but if he was going to go round my full-back, what was going to happen when we came up against Super League opposition?

Hampo had been my room-mate at five Wembley finals, but I had to do what I felt was best for the club. And that meant getting rid of him. A couple of weeks later, I called him into the office at the club and broke the news. He didn't accept it – I still don't think he does – and he told me as much. But I was the coach, I had made the decision, and there was no going back.

We all make mistakes, and I have made my fair share, but I was adamant that this was the right thing to do. As a coach, you are only as good as what's out on the field – although some of the stick that goes flying around amazes me. Towards the back end of my reign at Salford, you'd have thought I was telling the players to go out and drop the ball or miss tackles. I'm sure Kevin Keegan didn't say to Phil Neville in Euro 2000, 'Wait until two minutes from time, and then make a clumsy challenge to lose us the game.' I never did anything like that either, but when it all started going pear-shaped, the fingers were all pointing in my direction and no one else's. Okay, I got rid of a few popular players, like David Young and Richard Webster who both went back to Wales, but every decision I made was with the best interests of the club at heart.

Maybe if I had stayed as focused throughout as I was when I first took over, I would still be Salford coach – but we're all masters of hindsight, aren't we? Still, it was surprising how quickly I went from being one of the best coaches in the business in many people's eyes to one of the worst. Don't forget, in my first two seasons in charge at the Willows we won promotion, took the Premiership at Old Trafford, reached the Challenge Cup quarter-final where we got smashed by what was a great St Helens side, and capped it all by finishing fifth in Super League when everyone tipped us to go straight back down. It just goes to show how fickle rugby league fans can be. Less than two seasons after everyone was tipping me as the next Great Britain coach, I was apparently the devil incarnate at Salford.

You'd never have thought how it was going to turn out in February 1996 when, by the most ironic twist of fate, we were the team that sent Wigan to their first Challenge Cup defeat in eight years. No one gave us a prayer when we drew them, even though we were at home, and it was quickly built up into a fixture between Andy Gregory and his old club – even more so after we pulled off a fantastic victory. But as far as I was concerned, it wasn't about me, it was about my players. After all, I wasn't the one who sent Nathan McAvoy over for two tries; I wasn't the one who kicked the goals from the touch-line, and I wanted the players to get the recognition for their achievements. And while that obviously has to go down as one of the highlights of my coaching career, it didn't give me as much pleasure as winning the league twice on consecutive seasons and taking Salford into Super League. That only came after a whole string of good performances, rather than a one-off.

It's funny in hindsight, but when we had drawn them everyone thought I was just coming out with all the expected bravado when I said that I thought we could beat them. But that was honestly how I saw it. Their grip on the Cup had to slip at some stage, so why shouldn't it be Salford who beat them? That was how I saw it – and for once Mystic Greg was right!

It makes me laugh now to think that the same people who turned against me have at the same time been raving about the good young kids on the books at the Willows, such as Gary Broadbent, Stuart Littler, Malcolm Alker and Paul Southern. Maybe they don't realise who signed them in the first place. And before they had a go at me for selling players such as Scott Naylor, perhaps they should have taken the trouble to find out the true story. I had heard a rumour that Scott was going to sign for Bradford, so I asked him point blank about it. He categorically denied it and said he was staying put. But the next morning he came up and said he hadn't told me the truth. There was nothing I could do about it because he would shortly be out of contract, and if we didn't sell him now he would join the Bulls for nothing at the end of the season under the Bosman ruling. I copped a load of flak for selling Nathan McAvoy to Bradford at the same time for £100,000 – but that largely came about because Salford needed the money, it was as simple as that.

John Wilkinson also came in for some stick over that, among other things, but the harsh reality is that if it weren't for him, the club would quite possibly not exist. John might not be everyone's cup of tea, but he and I worked very well together, and I have a lot of time for him. One of the most memorable occasions of my coaching career came when I had the great honour of taking charge of Great Britain for the 1997 World Nines, and John came to Australia with me as manager. That was my choice, as was the physio Linda Atherton, who had helped me play in three Challenge Cup finals when I was really struggling for fitness.

My squad selection was hindered somewhat by a ruling that stated I could only take one player from each club. Even so, we won all our pool games, including New Zealand, who were the second favourites, before eventually losing in the sem-final. But that had given me a taste of coaching on an even bigger stage, and I really enjoyed the experience. I firmly believe that if I hadn't had all the problems that later took over my life, then I would have gone on to become the next Great Britain coach. That's not a big-headed boast; it was something that everyone was tipping to happen. Little was I to know that things were about to take a dramatic turn for the worse.

Now I have always had my run-ins with referees, but it reached the stage when I was coach of Salford where I thought all the 50–50 decisions were going against me. The Rugby Football League denied it, but it's funny that of all the players and coaches who came out with comments criticising referees in the heat of the moment, I was the only one who ever seemed to get dragged in to answer charges of bringing the game into disrepute. You see and hear of a million players and coaches swearing from the sidelines or out in the middle, and I was no different. But when I blew my top at Steve Ganson during one televised match, and the cameras and microphones picked it up, that was me, up in front of the Rugby Football League once again. I was fined £1,500 and banned from the touch-line, which was ridiculous – especially when three other coaches after me all publicly slated officials, and all of them got off with a slap on the wrist. If that wasn't a witch-hunt against Andy Gregory, then I don't know what was.

When they banned me from the touch-line I would have quit there and then, if it hadn't been for my maintenance payments. I seriously considered packing it all in 12 months before I eventually did, but the fact was that I couldn't afford it. In hindsight I wish I had, because then I wouldn't have had to suffer the most disappointing defeat of my entire career. When we lost to St Helens in the 1997 Challenge Cup semi-final, the result was known well before the end of the game because they were so far ahead. But the following season, just reaching the semi-final wasn't enough. We were playing Sheffield Eagles for a place at Wembley and, with all due respect to our opponents, we went into the game at Headingley firmly believing that we were on course for a weekend in London as Challenge Cup finalists. Everything went according to plan, too. We were on top for most of the game, we were the better team, and we basically had it won. But a few minutes before the end they went over for the match-winning try, and our Wembley dream was shattered in the most heartbreaking of circumstances.

I know I'd had my disagreements with John Wilkie in the past, but I would have loved to have given him the chance to walk out at the head of his team at Wembley. Sadly it was not to be, as the door had been slammed in our face just as we were about to stroll through it. That dressing-room was probably the worst I have ever been in. There was just nothing I could say – everyone was gobsmacked and sat around in total silence. As usual people wanted a scapegoat for the defeat, and they didn't look any further than yours truly. I had opened a pub the night before the semi, and for some reason they seemed to think that was the reason for us losing. I don't know what it had to do with anything, but it was apparently a good enough excuse for them to have another go at me.

It all started going downhill from that day – and some of the things that went on were so petty that you wouldn't believe them. I began getting letters from the club secretary about my comments after games – this from the same club who had told me to try to get as much publicity for them as I could. As it was, I was fed up with being the biggest name on the books. I wanted the players to take all the credit, I would have loved them to have the headlines in the newspapers, and it wasn't my doing that the press only ever seemed to want to interview me.

The most ridiculous episode involved a game at the Willows when I was not even there in a working capacity. I used to go and watch the Academy and A team games, but left the team selection and coaching to my assistants and I didn't interfere at all. But I would go along with my Dalmatian, Hatti, and we would stand on the terraces – and when we were winning, everything was fine. All of a sudden, however, as soon as the results started going wrong, I started getting letters telling me my behaviour was unprofessional. And after one A team game against Bradford, I got a letter telling me that I wasn't to go again if I was going to take the dog with me! That really upset her, I can tell you, because she used to love watching the Bulls!

Then I got another rap on the knuckles about my dress code after we had played Gateshead away. Usually, when I stood on the sidelines, everyone recognised me because I had my waistcoat on, and my suit and tie. Certainly no one could ever accuse me of being scruffy. Before this game, however, I decided to change: I wore a Salford top, Salford shorts, and a Salford cap because I wanted to try to build the team spirit up, and I went out for the warm-up with the lads dressed like that. But the next day I got a letter telling me that my dress was not good enough for a Super League coach. You saw other coaches wearing the same as me, and nothing was ever said. And it wasn't as though I had run out with a Manchester United hat on – everything I was wearing was Salford.

That highlighted to me the fact that they were simply looking for excuses. By that stage everything I did was wrong, and they were just trying to force me through the door. It all came to a head 24 hours after what should have gone down as one of the best days of my life, when I had been given the tremendous honour of being one of only four people named in the Wigan club's Hall of Fame. Salford were playing at Bradford at tea-time, and earlier in the day I had gone to Central Park for the official dinner. It was a great occasion for my family and me, and I went along with Mavis – the friend who had got me that first job at GUS – Derek Birchall, Cliff Fleming, Salford director Neil Hilton, brother Bryn and my mum. From there I got straight on to the team coach to travel to Odsal, where we put in a terrible performance and lost quite heavily. Little did any of us know that on Salford's next visit to Bradford, with a different coach, they would have 96 points put past them.

Immediately after the final whistle, I rang my bank manager at home on my mobile phone from the side of the pitch and asked him whether he thought I could afford to quit. He told me I couldn't – but my life was going downhill faster than Franz Klammer, and I just couldn't take any more. If I had tried, I think I would have cracked up completely.

When people talk about mixed emotions, I don't think you could get a better example than mine that day. I had been so happy at lunchtime at Central Park, but I had ended the afternoon watching my players miss tackles, knock on, kick the ball out on the full . . . I had gone from the Hall of Fame to the Hall of Shame in about six hours. On the coach coming home I had a word with Wilkie and asked him if he could afford to pay me half my money, because I had had enough. John told me that he would have a think about things over the next few days, but my mind was already made up.

A lot of the true Salford fans knew that I was going through all sorts of hell. But instead of getting behind the team, all they wanted to do was to give me even more. It proved to me again how fickle people could be. I think what disappointed me the most was that no one would say what they thought to my face.

It got so bad that some players I had released back to amateur clubs thought it was a great laugh to ring me on the mobile and start abusing me and my family. That really was beyond a joke – although full credit to their clubs – who stepped in and put a stop to that straightaway.

It sounds like I am having a go at everything connected with Salford, but nothing could be further from the truth. There are a lot of people there who worked damned hard, like Andrew Bentham, the commercial manager, and Paula and Christine in the office. If everyone put as much into the club as they did, Salford would be up there with the best in Super League.

I had still said nothing publicly about my decision to resign – I left that to John Wilkinson. But when the news finally broke, John's versions of events was that Salford had terminated my contract. Or, to put it another way, I had been sacked. That wasn't the case, but to argue about it would only have been splitting hairs. My heart wasn't in it, and Wilkie knew it. As he told me himself, he wanted me back to the old cocky, chirpy Andy Gregory who had first arrived at the club. It's been one hell of a hard road, but at last I feel that I am getting there now.

FOURTEEN

Lauren

I first met Dawn during my early days as a player with Widnes. She used to go along to Naughton Park quite a lot when her dad, Tony Karalius, was still playing. He had played at Wembley, and was acknowledged as one of Great Britain's finest. Her uncle, the great Vince Karalius, had as good a reputation if not better, so there was a strong rugby league connection in her family well before I came along. In fact, in comparison with the fame and glory that Vince and Tony had enjoyed, I was hardly a big-time star – not as a teenage hopeful who was working as a pan-scrubber at GUS – even though I had just about broken into the Widnes first team by then. Anyway, we started courting, things progressed and we had a great wedding.

Life was great in those days. We had money, cars, nice houses, and everything was going well. Not that we needed bundles of cash to enjoy ourselves. I remember the time when we were living in Grappenhall, and I was in dispute with the club, and we just about had enough to buy some groceries.

A lot of water has passed under the bridge since those days, but I still look back on them fondly. I know I am not the only person in the world to have made mistakes and got divorced, but to this day how I did it was wrong; I upset a lot of people. I simply didn't think what I was doing, or what would it do to those who had been close to me and around me for years. It was the typical Andy Greg syndrome – not listening to anything that anyone said to me. I was totally wrapped up in my own little world, and no one could get through to me or get any sense out of me.

One thing I always wanted was to be a good dad to Lauren, my little girl. But in my playing days I was away a lot on Great Britain tours, or down in London for the various Wembley finals. If it wasn't something on the field then I would be off making a personal appearance somewhere, and there were times when I was hardly ever at home.

I did spend some time with Lauren, of course. What she really loved doing was walking the dogs, or going swimming. And Dawn has got a lovely picture of her sitting on my shoulders at St Pat's. Those are memories that I will never, ever lose, whatever may happen in the future. But I am thoroughly embarrassed and ashamed to admit that, after I split up with Dawn, there were times when I should have gone over to pick Lauren up, and I was in the pub instead.

That doesn't stop me being very, very proud of her. She is a very bright girl, with a cracking sense of humour. Okay, maybe she was fortunate in that we could afford to buy her computers and the like from a very early age, but a lot of the credit for her doing so well at school isn't down to that: it is down to the work Dawn has put in with her over the years. Everyone who knows

Dawn and I realises that we have had our ups and downs, and perhaps we will never see eye to eye on everything. But one thing I will never, ever doubt is her ability as a mother. She is absolutely in the top bracket in that respect.

There are certain things that Lauren has been told about me which I don't like or accept, but the people who have done that know who they are, and she is a bright enough kid to make her own mind up in time. One day, when she is old enough, I will sit her down and talk to her about everything. I know damn well that I have let her down, and no one is more ashamed about that than me. If I could turn the clock back I would do, but all I can do is to make sure I don't repeat my mistakes over the years ahead. And if Dawn and myself can speak and be civil to each other – and I have no reason to doubt that we can – then I am sure we will work something out that will suit us all.

Lauren will only have been about ten when Dawn and I split up, and I really regret that she had to listen to the shouting which went on between two grown-ups. If you can call us such, that is, because there were times when I think she was the most adult of the three of us.

I still remember the Wednesday when Dawn telephoned me at the scrapyard in tears. I just told Tony that I was off. He asked me what was going on, but all I could say was, 'I don't know – I'll have to call you later.' He was as worried as me because, don't forget, this was his daughter we're talking about here. I hadn't a clue what was going on, but I rushed home to Grappenhall, and as soon as I walked through the door Dawn told me she was expecting. With the sole exception of the actual birth itself, that will remain the happiest day of my life.

The day that surpassed it came on 3 March 1987, when Lauren was born in Warrington General Hospital. I was working in the scrapyard again, and I rushed home as fast as possible and immediately went to the hospital. Everything went smoothly, and I made the traditional calls to my mum and my mother-in-law to break the news that we had a baby girl. Then I went out to wet the baby's head.

Having seen what Dawn went through to give birth, I vowed at the time never to complain again about playing rugby, whatever injuries I picked up along the way. She certainly had to do it tough – but when we got Lauren, it was well worth it. And before any women have a go at me, I know it is very easy to say that from my point of view. But it is an awful feeling when you know you are so helpless, unable to do anything for them.

From a very early age with Lauren it was always Dad this and Dad that, and the fact that I am not there for her all the time is something that I don't think I will ever totally manage to come to terms with. But she will always know who her dad is, and she will always know that he is there for her, whatever the problems, whatever the time, wherever she is.

It's been three years now since Dawn and I split up, and we tend to go through phases. There was a time when I couldn't see Lauren for a while, but recently things seem to have been sorted out a little better, and I hope that will carry on. I lost an awful lot in the divorce, but I won't lose sight of the fact that I have a beautiful daughter who means the world to me. I know the divorce was my fault, but I will start again. And I am not wallowing in self-pity here, because although I know it has been tough for me – and it still is – Lauren and Dawn have hardly had the easiest of times either. But I am sure that we can patch up our differences, and there is nothing I would like better than to have a nice little house where Lauren can stay over with me.

When I went through the phase of not having a lot of contact, it wasn't just me who was affected; it used to break my mother's heart as well, what with her being Lauren's grannie and not seeing her. Bryn, my brother, and his wife Sharon have two lovely girls in Natalie and Danielle, and they all think the world of Lauren as well. I don't think it's fair that others should have to suffer like that, just because of the mistakes I made.

Despite everything, there have been good times. She is 13, I am 38, and I hope more than anything – in fact, I am sure – that there are many more good times for us to have together. I will prove to her that her dad is not a drunken bum – and that was probably one of the major factors in pulling me out of it all. Lauren has seen her dad playing rugby and she has seen him on TV. But by the same token, she has also seen the side that threatened to take over my whole life. But no matter what happens, she will never forget who her dad is. And for the right reasons as well.

Lauren used to love coming out for a walk with me and the dogs, she used to come to games from time to time, and she loves horses. In fact, she said from a young age that she wanted to be a vet, and although that is a very, very tough profession to get into, if anyone can make it she can.

I know everyone says this about their own kids, but I think she is very, very special. The main thing is that Lauren knows it as well. Believe me, it is true.

FIFTEEN

Stars in my Eyes

Rugby league has been good to me in a number of ways, not least that it had led to me meeting countless stars from other sports. There is no way that a young lad from Lower Ince could ever have dreamed about even rubbing shoulders with some of the people I am proud to call friends.

There have also been more than a few laughs along the way. I remember one night in particular being in a restaurant in Worsley with a mate, when Ryan Giggs turned up. He was just beginning to make a real name for himself at Manchester United, and when he spotted me he came over to the table and chatted for about ten minutes. Ryan is a rugby league fan, and knows a lot about the game because his dad, Danny, used to play at Swinton. We were talking about rugby, United – don't forget, I am huge supporter of the Reds – and Wales. In fact, that's when it hit home to me how proud he was to play for the Welsh. After a while he headed off to his own table, and someone leaned over and asked, 'Wasn't that Ryan Giggs?' I don't know how I kept my face straight when I replied sarcastically 'Yes, it was, he's a real mithering b*****d at times, isn't he?'

It was only said in fun, and Ryan would realise that, but I am so impressed by the way he has handled everything. A lot of the credit for that has to go down to Alex Ferguson, his manager, and his mother. There have been times when I wish I'd had them helping me as well.

Alex has always been great to me. The day after we had beaten Wigan in the Challenge Cup during my time as Salford coach, the telephone rang at home and Lauren answered it. The phone had been going all morning after the memorable events of the previous day, and when I asked her who it was, she said it was some bloke called Ferguson. She didn't miss many United games back then, so her face was an absolute picture when I picked up the receiver and shouted to her that Fergie was on the line.

I used to go all over the place to watch United, and during one European Cup run I went to see them play Porto away with Neil Hilton, one of the Salford directors. When Alex came around to the side of the pitch to take his position on the bench, he spotted me in the crowd and called me down. He was just minutes away from a vitally important European quarter-final, but he still took the trouble to wish me all the best in our Challenge Cup semi-final against St Helens that weekend. As it turned out, we got flogged, but that was by the by.

On another occasion Steve Hampson and I had been invited to the Ryder Cup at the Belfry as guests of De Vere. The drive down had been a real laugh, although we knew that it meant one of us not having a drink if we were to get back that night. Play started late because of fog, and by the time it had finished it had been a really long day, so we decided to have a couple with the intention of sleeping in the car. We teamed up with cricketers Neil Fairbrother and Mike Atherton, who had accommodation, albeit in a caravan. We carried on having a good time, moved on to the nightclub at the Belfry, and ended the night on the caravan floor with Athers and Harvey. Next day we made an early start, watched a bit more golf, and then headed for home. We might not have slept in the most salubrious place in the world, but it was a memorable trip none the less.

Only last year, a mate of mine called Trevor Lloyd invited me down to the British Grand Prix as a guest of Mobil. I had never really been a big fan of Formula 1, but we went down to the pits to meet David Coulthard and Mika Hakkinen, and it really opened my eyes to see the money and real wealth that was involved in the sport. There have also been trips to the Cheltenham Gold Cup, to Aintree for the Grand National, and numerous big cricket matches.

I know the head groundsman at Lancashire, Peter Marron, very well and on one occasion he got us tickets for a Test match against Australia at Lord's. It turned out that they were for the press box, but that didn't bother us. All we wanted to do was get into the ground, and watch the cricket with a few beers. When we arrived in the press enclosure, we came across the perfect example of a little Hitler. He epitomised the phrase, 'Give a man a uniform and he'll cause trouble anywhere'. He demanded to know where we had got the tickets from, and although we told him that we didn't even want to sit with the press, we just wanted to watch the cricket, he began to get very obnoxious. So I eventually had a quiet word in his ear, if you get my meaning, and for five minutes or so he left us alone. But as we made to leave the press box to find a seat, another bloke came up and started giving us more grief. By then I'd had enough, and I told him what I would do to him if he didn't go away. How was I to know that I had just threatened to knock the block off the chairman of the TCCB?

The head groundsman at Lord's got wind of all this and quickly phoned Peter at Lancashire. Peter came on the line and said, 'Whatever you do, don't hit him, Andy – he's one of the most important men in English cricket, and you are in the press box.' What the assembled journalists made of it all, I don't know. But at least we got some seats and spent the rest of the day in peace.

There have been some memorable occasions with the boxing fraternity as well. One of the best came after I met a guy called Johnny Lewis on the 1988 Great Britain tour to Australia, and he introduced me to Jeff Fenech. Jeff was a world champion, and I met him again when I had that spell with Illawarra. I said that I'd love to go and see him fight if ever he was in Europe, but thought little more of it until I got a call to tell me that he was lined up to meet Azumah Nelson in the Mirage Hotel, Las Vegas. Now I know that isn't in Europe, but does that really matter? I didn't really think there was a chance of getting the nod to go, but Dawn agreed, so I set off with Joe Lydon for ten days over in the States. We had a whale of a time – a round of golf, a trip to Wet And Wild, and we even flew down the Grand Canyon in a six-seater plane – which was unbelievable. Then we warmed up for the main event by going to see James 'Lights Out' Toney fight Michael Nunn on the Friday.

The following night was the biggie. We had fantastic seats, right by the ringside, and we couldn't believe it when the likes of Marvin Hagler, Leon Spinks and Thomas Hearns, not to mention countless Hollywood stars, took their seats around us. Jeff was fighting on the undercard to Mike Tyson's clash with Riddick Bowe, and it was an unforgettable experience. Jeff's fight went the distance, but everyone knew he had won it. Everyone except promoter Don King, that is, so naturally his opponent came out of it with a draw. That contest was voted the

1989 Fight of the Year by all the boxing writers, so it was a privilege to see it at such close quarters.

Next up it was Tyson, and from the moment he came through the curtains and into the arena, we were treated to the comments of the loudest-mouthed American idiot you could wish to meet. This Yank plank never stopped abusing Tyson from the second he appeared, and carried on shouting and bawling throughout the fight. In fact, if Tyson had heard him, I'm sure he'd have come over and knocked him out. I felt like doing it myself after about three rounds. That fight also went the distance, and Tyson got the verdict – much to the American joker's annoyance. By then he was really getting on my nerves, and I know he was having the same effect on Joe, because of what happened next. To this day Joe insists that I was the man responsible, but he and I both know that it was him. The loudmouth went to the toilets and had the misfortune to bump into Joe while he was there. Joe looked him up and down and said, 'I have come 6,000 miles to watch the fight, and you have almost spoiled my trip.' With that he knocked him out with the best right hook I saw that weekend.

As we walked back through the hotel, Joe tapped me on the shoulder and told me to look to my right. I couldn't believe my eyes when I saw Steven Spielberg playing cards with Bruce Willis, with Demi Moore standing behind him. It was a bit disappointing when she didn't look back, so we kept on walking – I wonder if she knows what she missed out on.

I'm pretty keen on the big boxing fights, and have also been to a couple of Chris Eubank's. I went to see the weigh-in for his scrap with Nigel Benn, with Richie Eyres, the former Leeds and Widnes player. Nigel was standing there with half a coconut in his hand, and Richie asked me what on earth I thought he was doing with it. I said, 'I've no idea, but if you're planning on taking it off him, wait until I'm out of the building.'

My rugby league fame once got me a slot on *A Question of Sport*, as a member of Ian Botham's team. I was actually scheduled to record the show the day after the second Ashes Test in 1990, which we had lost to a try in the final minute. I was gutted and had had a late night, and as soon as we arrived at the studio on the Sunday the bar opened. But after downing a few the night before, I knew it wouldn't take much to get me going again, so I made the wise choice to walk around Manchester for a while instead.

The thing that struck me about *A Question of Sport* was Botham. If you believed half the things you heard about him, you'd think he was some sort of monster – but he was a really genuine, down-to-earth guy who took a genuine interest and also knew his rugby. Mickey Skinner is another who gets a rough deal from people, even though they know nothing about him. I met Mickey a couple of times at *The Sun* Christmas party, when I was doing a column for the paper, and I have got a lot of time for the bloke. He is a top guy, a really genuine man and excellent company.

Everyone knows that me and referees get on about as well as turkeys and Christmas, so perhaps it may seem surprising that I am such good pals with Neil Midgley. But then again, maybe it doesn't really count because he was a football official; otherwise, things might have been different. One night I went to watch Tranmere play Luton at Prenton Park, and Midge was referee. At half-time I knocked on the officials' door and asked to see him. The usual Jobsworth went through the old routine of 'who are you, what do you want, you shouldn't be here', but he eventually told Neil that there was a short, stocky fellow asking for him who he thought played rugby. Midge called me in, and we ended up having a really good natter. The players must have been wondering what the hell was going on, because they ended up having a 25-minute half-time! Eventually I said to him, 'Don't you think you had better start?' and he just replied, 'Sod 'em, they're not going to do it without me.'

One of my biggest mates is a guy called Phil Lynch, who is an absolute Liverpool nut, and he got Robbie Fowler to come down to Newton-le-Willows when I was running the Bluebell there. Ian Rush is another who I've had numerous laughs with. He's also earned me a few quid as well, like the time he gave me four winners at York races. Thanks, Rushie! All these people have reached the pinnacle of their respective sports, but all of them have remained level headed and are genuinely nice people.

I've also had some great nights with Mark Hughes, the former Manchester United footballer, but he won't get me back in his car in a hurry. He once gave me a lift from Old Trafford to a hotel in Wilmslow in his brand-new white Porsche. On the face of it, it should have been a trip to remember. For me, however, we couldn't get there quick enough, because all he seemed to have to listen to in the car was a bloody Tom Jones tape!

There are lots of people from Old Trafford who have been good to me over the years, and chairman Martin Edwards is another. He has been a big fan of rugby league for years and years, to the extent that one year he even asked me if it was possible to come to the party after one of Wigan's Challenge Cup wins. He came along, and we all had a great night. Sunderland manager Peter Reid is another from the football world who knows his rugby league. I remember driving all the way up to Roker Park with Lauren on a foggy Wednesday night to see United play Sunderland in an FA Cup replay, after drawing 2–2 at Old Trafford. Peter had actually got us the tickets, and before the game he invited us into his office. Lauren was very young at the time, and she decided to practise her writing on the steamed-up windows. It was just unfortunate that she wrote 'I love Man United' in huge letters. Reidy, to his credit, just fell about laughing.

Considering rugby union and rugby league were supposed to be at each other's throats during my playing days, the men in the thick of it on the field were good pals. During my time at Illawarra in 1989 the British Lions were on tour in Australia, and I got to know scrum-half Robert Jones pretty well. I was well chuffed when they beat the Aussies in Sydney, and I went into the dressing-room after the match. I agreed with Robert to trade a Lions shirt for a Great Britain one – but 11 years on, we've still not got round to swapping them!

After seeing how these people from other sports were with fans, I never refused an autograph. Not that I had done previously, to be honest, although some in the game haven't always been the best in that department. That was the one thing that really disappointed me during the late 1980s, when Wigan was conquering the world and the sport of rugby league had the ideal opportunity to push itself and get some much-needed publicity. We had the Great Britain manager at Central Park, as well as the Great Britain captain. So I can't explain why, or believe how, Ellery Hanley was allowed to get away without speaking to the press. It simply would not happen in any other sport.

I remember Ellery refusing point blank to do one interview at Wembley; Maurice Lindsay turned to me and asked me to do it in his place. I duly did the business, but was disillusioned by what Ellery could get away with. Fair enough, he made his choice not to co-operate with the media, and got a rough deal off some of the news reporters in return. And in many ways I don't blame Ellery at all – but I do blame the Wigan and Great Britain management for allowing him to get away with it. I couldn't have imagined Alan Shearer being asked to do an interview to publicise Euro 2000, turning it down flat, and no one saying a word about it. If Gary Lineker, Will Carling or Mike Atherton had all refused to speak to the media, do you think they would have got away as lightly?

Here we were, the most successful team in the history of the game, in a sport that was crying out desperately for as much publicity as it could get. But what did we do? We allowed one of the few names that broke down north-south barriers to get away with his wish of not speaking to the media. That really disappointed me about rugby league – I guess it always will.

SIXTEEN

Summer You Win, Some You Lose

Rugby League's switch to summer in 1996 has caused more arguments than any other development in the game over recent years – and I have to admit that even now I still have the odd doubt. If you did a survey among the players, however, there would be no argument. I think that they all, to a man, are in favour of it.

One thing it has led to, though, is an increase in cheating and gamesmanship. I don't mean a rise in cheap shots and sly digs, but little things that the average fan maybe wouldn't even notice. How many times do you see someone running on from the sidelines with a water bottle? I'm sure that the vast majority of people believe that he is passing on instructions from the coach – unless, of course, he is giving fluids to a player. That may be the case on certain occasions, but quite often the reason is a lot more than that: it's to take his place as an extra defender. If your winger and centre are leaving a gap, or a hole is constantly appearing up the middle, the water carrier will run on to fill it. Any player with any skill only needs to spot the slightest opening, and he is through it. But the ball-carrier makes decisions in the heat of the moment, and if he spots a body in what he thought was a gap out of the corner of his eye – be it an opponent, the referee or a water-carrier – then it makes him hesitate for a split second, and the chance is invariably lost. With the water-carriers, all you are trying to do is distract the opposition for an instant. In a way that is cheating, and I have done it as a coach as well – everyone does.

That's not to say that there aren't occasions when players do need fluids on the field of play. As I have already explained, I don't think I ever took on water during a match – in England, at least – but these days I am sure that even I would need a drink at some stage. I've played in the heat of Papua New Guinea, and I know how oppressive that can be. A hot summer's day in Wigan or Castleford might not compare with Port Moresby, but it can still be bloody warm, and it can be very dangerous if your water levels drop too low.

One thing that does worry me and plays strongly on my mind about the modern game is the skill level. I was very fortunate in my playing career, because I would say that about 98 per cent of it was successful; I was in great teams picking up trophies every season. Despite all the honours, I know that I probably came up with plenty of errors, purely and simply because as a scrum-half and playmaker I touched the ball more than anyone else – but by and large I don't think I did a bad job. Yet if you look at the top teams these days, I firmly believe you will struggle to come up with a top-class British scrum-half who can cut the mustard at the highest level. I know there are plenty of promising lads out there, but it's one thing doing it each week in domestic club rugby, and another level entirely when you are playing for your country.

How many times has the same situation cropped up in football? Our club game in the Premiership is probably as strong as any in the world – although it is packed with foreigners. And we saw at Euro 2000 how difficult it is for the English players to make that additional step up to the higher level. I'm afraid that British rugby league is in for a rocky ride for the foreseeable future as well.

I watched New Zealand play Australia recently and was amazed when the Kiwis got a right old thrashing. The really frightening thing about that is the prospect of England facing the Aussies: New Zealand gave a unified Great Britain team a beating the last time we met – what would the world champions do to a side shorn of its Welshman, Scots and Irish? The thought doesn't bear thinking about, and the reality is that it could set the international game back years. Believe me, rugby league at the highest level could do with a mighty boost at the moment. That's why I was so desperate for the 2000 Rugby League World Cup to be a success, especially in the light of England's failure at Euro 2000. Yet however much progress we may be making – if indeed we making any – it hardly increased our chances in the tournament to split Great Britain into the home nations.

There are many aspects of our game that have improved over recent years, but I honestly believe that the emphasis on statistics has masked a number of problems. As a player I never needed anyone to come up to me at 4.30 on a Sunday afternoon and tell me whether I'd done well or not. Of course, I would take on board various points made by my coach and certain of my team-mates, but no way did I need to look at a stats sheet to see how I had played. These days, though, there is so much credence given to numbers of busts, drives, big hits and yardage that I think a lot of the time players aren't allowed to be honest with themselves any more. Some of them will come off thinking, 'I had a shocker today'; but then they will look at the stats and go home believing that they didn't do too badly after all. I'm not saying that statistics and suchlike don't have a place in the game, but there is a danger of overkill.

It all comes back to the skill factor. Take the ball-playing forward, for example: a few years ago the game was awash with them. From the days of Mal Reilly, through Brian Lockwood, Knocker Norton and Lee Crooks, every team seemed to have a couple. I know there is the odd one or two knocking about now, but nothing like the numbers we used to boast in the days when Great Britain were on a par with Australia.

One of the best I ever saw was Doug Laughton – which got me a real ticking-off once during my early career with Widnes. I was only a young lad, and during an interview someone asked me who I'd looked up to as a kid. To be honest, I hadn't had any real heroes when I was still dreaming of life as a pro, but Roger Millward had always quite impressed me, so I came up with his name. Before the next game Doug sidled up and whispered in my ear, 'I don't know whether to pick you this week, you little so-and-so, because you came up with the wrong answer – it should have been me, without hesitation!'

There also seemed to be a lot more fun in the game in previous years. There was certainly nothing like the row between BARLA and the Rugby Football League which has done the game nothing but harm over the past 20 years. We should all be pulling in the right direction and trying to take the sport forward. Much of the blame for the friction between amateurs and professionals has to be placed at the door of the scouts. These days you hear of professional clubs signing players as young as 12 or 13 – I have seen it happen with my own eyes.

Some clubs try to snap up players who show the merest hint of talent purely and simply to stop anyone else getting them. Then when it becomes obvious that the kid isn't up to it, he is classed as a failure. Instead of going back to the amateur game, he is lost to rugby league for good. Naturally, there will always be exceptionally talented youngsters, but they certainly don't occur in the numbers that are signed up nowadays.

We must get the young kids coming through again. Towards the end of my days as Salford coach I never even bothered to send anyone to scout BARLA matches, because I knew there just wasn't anyone coming through. When I was a teenager, sides like Wigan St Pat's, Widnes St Marie's, Crosfields, Leigh Miners . . . they were all packed with good young prospects. For some reason you just don't see that any more.

Another thing that gets my goat is all the talk of expansion. I am all for rugby league breaking down barriers, but we have to ask whether it has really worked in London, for example. Was it really a success in France, when Paris had their brief sspell in Super League? The one place where I believe we have totally missed the boat is South Wales. Believe me, that really is a hotbed of rugby league. People still only seem to class it as a rugby union area, but I have got a lot of mates down there, and they are very much fans of both codes. I have been lucky enough to visit Cardiff Arms Park and the Millennium Stadium for various sporting events, and I know that while they love their union, they are very passionate about league as well. Just look at the numbers who used to head north each week when the likes of Jonathan Davies, Allan Bateman and John Devereux were playing professionally. I have seen all the hard work that has gone on in the past to try to establish a team there, and I reckon that eventually the game's rulers will see sense, support them properly and give them a Super League franchise – I certainly hope so.

We see administrators jetting off to America to try to give rugby league a foothold over there, but they are wasting their time. I should know; I played for Wigan against Warrington in a challenge game in Milwaukee, and the interest simply isn't there on a big enough scale. Instead of looking at places like that, we should be concerning ourselves with strengthening rugby league in Lancashire, Yorkshire and Cumbria. As soon as those particular houses are well in order, the rest will follow. And it is a disgrace that we don't have a strong Cumbrian team. When you look at the great names who have come from that area, it is appalling to think what has happened to their professional clubs.

I don't go along with those who blame Rupert Murdoch and Sky for the current state of the game. After all, if News Corporation hadn't come along when they did, rugby league might not even be here now. Yet aren't we in danger now of heading back in the same direction? Ask any club chairman or secretary if anyone in the game is making money apart from the players – who, I hasten to add, I do not attach any blame to. If your chairman tells you he is going to give you a contract worth £80,000 a year, you are not going to turn round and tell him to drop it by 20 grand because the club might not be able to afford it. The simple truth is clubs are offering money to players that they can't afford to pay.

And as for all the big plans contained in 'Framing the Future', which were supposed to improve just about every aspect of the game – what on earth happened to them? It is all well and good to see arenas being developed like the JJB Stadium or the McAlpine, but it all comes down to the big question – are we actually making any money? Every year we seem to come up with different criteria for clubs to fulfil to get into Super League. Does anyone ever stick to them? And does every club comply with the salary cap, which was designed to stop them plunging into a financial black hole once again?

When I first signed for Widnes, I thought rugby league was a professional game run by amateurs. To be honest, not much has really changed in that respect, while rugby union has come on in leaps and bounds. Just look at the respective media coverage the two sports get. I feel sorry that league can't compete with the rival code in terms of TV time or column inches, but it must sort out its publicity machine.

Full credit to Maurice Lindsay, who seems to be everyone's favourite punchbag as far as rugby league is concerned. Only recently, now that he is back as chairman of Wigan, he copped another load of flak for signing a couple of top Australians on big contracts. But that won't bother Maurice – he's been down that road before, and he'll just laugh off all the criticism. The man is a great talker, and there have been plenty of times when I think he should have been a politician. All he said on this occasion was that when other clubs joined the race and signed some top players of their own, he would be the first to congratulate them. Leeds duly followed suit, and Maurice duly paid tribute to them for it. Class!

I have had my run-ins with him over the years, but I reckon he made the decision that saved this game by agreeing the Murdoch deal in 1995. What everyone else must do is make sure they have learn the lessons of previous years. If you are running a business, and let's face it, that is what rugby league is now – then you have to get people through the door and make it enjoyable for them. It doesn't matter how good the pre-match entertainment is, what really counts is the 80 minutes of action. Clubs have got to have success on the field to be a success off it – and there are only a few who can manage that. While I do believe the skill levels have dropped in recent times, I am also convinced that when you have two sides flogging each other in a good old-fashioned local derby, there isn't a better game in the world.

Training ideas in the British game have bucked up a lot since I first started, but there is no doubt that the Southern Hemisphere sides have a big advantage over us because of the sun on their backs. Believe me, it is a damn sight easier going through a session on the beach at Surfers' Paradise than it is at a freezing cold Naughton Park, with the smell of burning carcasses from the Grannocks drifting across the Runcorn–Widnes Bridge.

We saw how far ahead of us the Aussie clubs were in the World Club Championship in 1997. I think everyone accepted before the competition began that the winners would come from Down Under, and that our sides would struggle to match them. But I must admit it was a shock to see how badly the British clubs did en masse, because I honestly felt that some of our bigger names would at least give them a game. At the end of the day, the Aussies are just too good. That hurts like hell to say, but I am afraid it is true.

At least some of our clubs do seem to have learned a lesson from that, and Bradford Bulls are the prime example. Carl Jennings, their fitness conditioner, has really brought them on a ton, so much so that if they held another World Club Championship this season, I reckon the Bulls would push a lot of Aussie sides close. One of the big differences has been that, in Australia, the clubs haven't just looked one season ahead, they have planned for two, three or even four years down the track. Now our top sides are doing likewise, and that will only benefit our game in the long run.

And while I do think the skill level has gone down noticeably in British rugby league on a collective basis, individually we have some flair players who can cut it with the best. Take Iestyn Harris, for example – although I have to admit that I still don't know where his best position is. He is possibly the best back in the British game right now, but if I was still coaching I think I'd struggle to say for definite whether he should be playing full-back or stand-off. I think he could be the man who Great Britain eventually build their team around. If we can produce a good number seven to line up with him and Andy Farrell, who is our top loose forward, then I think Iestyn will eventually become a world-class stand-off. Then it all comes down to which of them is prepared to stand aside and let the other call the shots. At Wigan in the glory years, Ellery had a reputation as possibly the world's finest player, but he was always willing to stand aside and allow me to fulfil the playmaking role. When I wanted the ball, nine times out of ten I got it.

We have got to develop the players, and develop the system. Then – and only then – will we be on track to push the Aussies close again.

SEVENTEEN

The Crucial Three

Any side which aspires to even the slightest hint of success has got to work together as a team, no matter how great the individuals within it may be. And probably the most crucial partnership within any set-up concerns the stand off, scrum-half and loose forward. That was one of the main reasons we enjoyed such dominance at Wigan.

At Central Park we had three of the greats in Shaun Edwards at six, Ellery Hanley at 13 and – modesty permitting – myself at seven. During the mid to late 1980s, Ellery was widely accepted as one of the top three players in the world. Even the Aussies, who love nothing better than slagging off the Poms, admitted that. But for all his individual ability, Hanley was a team player first and foremost. That's why he was more than willing to stand aside and let me call the shots in that side. I used to call all the moves, and nine times out of ten when I demanded the ball, I got it.

It was the same story with Shaun, who went on to become the

most decorated player in the history of the game. Shaun and I got on tremendously well on the field, and he, Ellery and the rest of the lads knew that if I pulled off a move, and it helped us to pick up two more points or another trophy, then it would only enhance everyone's reputation. Someone has got to take the responsibility and be brave enough to back their own judgement to carry it through. Of course, there will be times when you upset people – often your own team-mates – along the way. But come 4.30 on a Sunday afternoon, it is all about coming off the pitch as a winner – and everyone at Central Park knew that.

It's amazing to look back now and think that there used to be stories floating around about how Shaun and I didn't get on. Well, I can tell you once and for all that they were absolute rubbish. If they had been true, do you honestly think we would have been able to link up and play together so well as a partnership? I don't think I am being big-headed when I say that neither Wigan nor Great Britain have ever really managed to replace us, whatever success each of them has enjoyed since. It will be a hell of a long time before any team comes up with a trio like us two and Ellery. Who knows, perhaps they never will.

Naturally there were times when we disagreed over things, but that was only down to the three of us having a burning desire to continue our winning run, and nothing else. There was certainly no truth in the rumours that, as soon as we were back in the dressing-room, there were blazing rows between us. Off the field I may not have seen eye to eye with Ellery over everything, but that is true of all people who work together. And so long as they get along in whatever their profession or business may be, then what does it matter? We never had any massive fall-outs. I went out for a few drinks after training with Shaun on numerous occasions, and we'd talk about tactics, big games coming up, the opposition or whatever. Ellery tended to go his own way and do his own thing. But come match-day I would put him through a gap, he would put the ball down over the whitewash and everyone would be happy.

People often think that because a team plays together, the players must live in each other's pockets – especially when you enjoy the success that we had at Wigan. But we all basically treated it as a job of work. Once the training session had finished, we would all head our different ways. There was nothing sinister in that, and it certainly wasn't because we hated the company of our team-mates. But if you work in a factory, no one expects you to clock off at the end of every day and then spend the whole night socialising with your workmates. Of course, there were variations to the rule, such as the season when we played eight games in 19 days to win the league title – but it was still a job, not a social club.

The one night we all went out together was a Thursday. In those days we used to get paid weekly, so most of us would head off for a drink after we had received our wages.

The thing with Ellery was that, although he was a great player, his biggest asset was his work rate. It really was phenomenal. He would be the first to admit that he wasn't the best passer of a ball, and he wasn't acknowledged as a great kicker – certainly, George Best had nothing to fear from him in that department. A lot of the time he would run sideways across the line, rather than shooting 50 yards forwards, but his great physical strength would invariably see him break through. And I have never come across anyone before or since who had a greater desire to win. Commitment, fitness, total dedication – he had the lot. The only person to run him close in terms of pushing himself to the limit was Dean Bell. I don't just mean in matches, but in every single training session. Shaun had his own ideas and warming-up methods and was just as dedicated, but in a different way. We all played through a lot of pain in our careers, but he carried on with some fearful knocks.

Perhaps the biggest compliment I ever received was an indirect one, in the form of a comment that Shaun once passed. He told a friend that he always wanted to play at scrum-half, and if the club ever bought someone to play in that position rather than him, he would not be happy. But he also added that he would not play stand-off to anyone other than me. Not that hearing this told me anything I didn't already know, because to this day I still believe I was a better scrum-half. I knew Shaun fancied playing at seven, and there were times when it did cause a little friction. But whatever may have been said or done in that respect, we still knew that when we walked out of the tunnel on a Sunday, we would both be giving 100 per cent to the cause.

I remember one particular trip to Wembley when we were going through the usual pre-match ritual of walking around the ground in our suits, soaking up the atmosphere. Shaun was captain, and Ray Stubbs from the BBC wanted to do an interview with us both on the pitch before the game. When the time came, Ray called us over and told Shaun that he was going to talk to him first. Shaun was totally relaxed, until the camera turned on to him and Ray said, 'It's a great day for a Wigan lad, leading out his hometown team,. Obviously you are hoping to pick up the Cup. How do you think it will go?' Shaun just turned to the camera and said, 'We are on a mission,' before turning away again. He wasn't being rude or obstructive; he was just absolutely focused on the job ahead. He was totally psyched up for the game and had real tunnel vision

In a way I feel a bit sorry for Shaun's younger brother, Billy-Joe. Their dad, Jackie, had been a great player before he was forced to retire with a back injury, while Shaun went on to win every medal in the game and captain his country, and he will go down as one of the greatest players rugby league has ever seen. So whenever his brother plays a game, everyone will be drawing comparisons, as unfair as that might be. I bet Ian Botham was delighted when Liam his son decided to concentrate on rugby union, rather than following his dad into cricket. Acts like that are impossible to follow, but people always expect you to.

When Dawn found out she was expecting, everyone was saying to me, 'I bet you want a lad so you can buy him his first pair of rugby boots.' I can honestly say that if we'd had a boy, I would have got him a tennis racket, a set of golf clubs, anything rather than that. There has to be an easier life than running around a rugby field with blokes trying to knock your head off. Then again, you can spend your whole life talking ifs and maybes. If Ellery had stayed at Bradford and I'd stuck with Widnes, who knows what would have happened? But the fact is, we both signed for a great Wigan side.

We all knew we were only as good as the players around us. We used to say that, in a team game, you are only as good as your weakest link – and it was a well-worn phrase around Central Park that if we had one weak link, it was one too many. There were plenty of times when we let someone know in no uncertain terms if we felt they weren't pulling their weight. There were plenty of players who found themselves on the receiving end of the rest of the team having a go at them for having been a passenger in one game or another. But the great thing about it was, whatever went on behind closed doors stayed that way.

I'd say that in those days I would be named Man of the Match about six times out of ten, but I used to throw all the prize-money in the kitty. All the sponsors who gave the awards would see was the man who went through a gap, or maybe the guy who had put him there. We called the forwards 'the pigs' because they did all the hard work in the middle of the field – and they were full of crap – while us prima donnas in the backs used to get all the headlines and glory. So it was only fair that we all had a share of the cash.

The team talks from Ellery was always really intense, but to be honest, he didn't really need to say anything. We all hated losing so much that we didn't need anyone to wind us up before we went out. It reached the stage where, if anyone so much as dropped a pass or put a kick in the wrong place during a training session, they would get a real rollicking. We were so focused that we wouldn't accept anything less than perfection. It's an old cliché, but we knew that every game was going to be like a cup-tie. The whole league wanted us to lose, and we were determined to disappoint them. Our goal at the start of every season was to go through it unbeaten. We knew it was nigh on impossible, but that was what we aimed for. We weren't big-headed, but we knew we were a bloody good side, and we just wanted to keep it all going. And all our opponents were always treated in the same way; we didn't class anyone above anyone else, because they were all as determined as each other to knock us over.

The players had their various nicknames as well, and coach John Monie came up with a classic for me that stuck throughout the rest of my Wigan days. We were in a team meeting when he turned to me and called me 'Speed Bump'. No one knew what he was on about, so he explained: 'You look at the video of our next match – when they run at Andy, he slows them down but he never stops anyone!'

John used to set us targets for each match – so many handling errors, so many penalties or whatever. He had worked out that if we made more than a set number of mistakes, we would probably get beaten. Maybe not by too many sides in this country, because we had the raw talent in the side to get by here

– but they weren't the standards by which John worked. He knew that if we faced a half-decent Australian side, they would really punish us for a high error count. If we missed, say, 16 tackles, came up with eight knock-ons and gave away half a dozen penalties, we would get turned over. He tried to instil that way of thinking into the whole side – it was just another example of the total professionalism that ran throughout the entire club.

We all knew that if we were out of the side for any length of time, then there was someone ready, willing and able to jump into our position. Maybe that's one of the reasons we all played on with knocks. Playing alongside Ellery, I saw him take some fearful hits, but I can't remember him ever showing it. People went out to try to knock him out of the game, but if they ever managed to hurt him he certainly wouldn't let them see it. He was one hell of a tough guy. Dean Bell was no soft centre either. If you told him to go and run through a wall, eventually he would batter his way to the other side. In his early days he had a lot of pace as well, and he and Ellery would sometimes leave the rest of us wincing at the regime they put themselves through in the gym.

While we weren't all the closest of friends socially, of course certain bonds were forged. My own was with Steve Hampson, who was – and still is – an absolutely top bloke. He missed out on three Challenge Cup finals through injury, but was still the happiest guy in town when I won the Lance Todd Trophy and Wigan lifted the Cup. There are some people I know who actually wanted their side to lose when they were out of the team – but not Steve.

Two of the unsung heroes of the line-up were Andy Platt and Martin Dermott. Platty was as solid as a rock and a real help to my game throughout my career. It was the same with Derms.

When you call a move, and the first pass from dummy-half is too high or low, by the time the ball gets out wide it will be on the floor and possession is given away. But the best passer of a ball from dummy-half that I ever saw was Martin, and at times it used to annoy me that people just didn't realise the quality of service he gave from acting half-back. That first pass is the most crucial of the lot, and Derms was the inspiration behind a lot of the tries we scored, without ever coming close to getting the praise he deserved.

Martin came into the side as hooker at the expense of Nicky Kiss, who was another real character. Nicky used to walk around the dressing-room before the match and bang you on the chest, hit you on the head, or whack you on the back. I think it was his way of psyching himself up, but he was absolutely mad. Half the knocks we picked up came from him before the game even kicked off.

I was lucky enough to play with some great centres over the years, but I think the best of the lot was Gene Miles. The fellow was a freak, an unbelievable player, and one of the finest signings Wigan ever made. I played against him when he was in the Aussie Test side and I am pleased I didn't have to come up against him regularly at club level. Gene was a different centre to Dean, and that season he had at Wigan in 1992 must have felt like a year of Christmas Days for Martin Offiah, he set up that many tries. Great player as Martin was, I think I'd have finished the season with about 30 touchdowns if I'd been playing inside Gene.

Which brings me on to Martin himself. If I listed all his great tries I'd need about another 100 pages, but one springs to mind as the best of the lot. And he scored some crackers. It came while he was still at Widnes, in a match against the touring Australians, when he got the ball behind his own line and ran diagonally across the field. He was chased all the way by Andrew Ettingshausen, one of the Aussie greats, but Martin left him for dead as he scored in the opposite corner. It was an absolutely incredible try.

For sheer pace I have never seen anyone to compare with Martin – that was what really made him the player he was. I used to laugh when I heard other teams shouting, 'Give it to Offiah – we'll knock his head off.' They had to catch him first. When it became clear that he was on his way to Central Park, it was a fantastic feeling. I don't think there has ever been a team you could rate as ten out of ten, but if we were an eight at the time, Martin turned us into a nine. Even though we saw him grab some great tries, he never ceased to amaze us with his ability. I have already said that he was the main reason why we won the Sydney Sevens, and some people only remember the long-distance efforts he got – but there was plenty more to his game than that. He was very similar to Stuart Wright, my old Widnes mate, in that respect – everyone called him Shirley because they thought he lacked a bit of courage. But the pair of them put their bodies on the line plenty of times.

Martin and Stuart both loved the big occasion, but perhaps the best big-game player of the lot was Joe Lydon. There were a number of matches when Joe would have been in the side anyway, but he was forced to switch to full-back to cover for the injured Hampo and did the job so well that he became Great Britain's first-choice number one. Everyone still talks about that famous day in the 1989 Challenge Cup semi-final at Maine Road, when Warrington were really putting us to the sword. They were well on top when someone threw the ball back, and Joe dropped a goal from inside his own half. As I realised what he was about to do I began to shout, 'What the f*** are you doing?' Before I'd got the words out I had changed it to, 'What a f***ing brilliant kick.' Joe gave me plenty of stick for that in the dressing-room afterwards, but it was the turning point of the whole match. Warrington were truly deflated, and we went on to victory and another Wembley triumph.

He pulled off something similar in a game at Halifax in the 1993 Challenge Cup quarter-finals during another Wembley run. It was a horrible day, freezing cold and snowing, and they were well on the way to knocking us out. We had dragged ourselves back into contention when Joe popped over another drop-goal, as cool as you like, seconds form the end to win the match. Admittedly it was from closer range than the one against Warrington, but it was just as crucial.

Despite all our success, we never dwelt on it. As soon as one victory was achieved, all we were concerned about was the next. We would go in and discuss the previous game on the Monday after it, but that was as far as it went – there was no basking in glory or talking of how great we were. It was our job, we all enjoyed it, and if we got well paid for it, then that just made us very lucky indeed.

People used to say that our dominance was no good for the game, but try telling that to the people in the Central Park dressing-room at the time. We were all determined to keep the run going, and we used to talk about it between those four walls virtually every day. We wanted everyone to hate us more and more, because that meant we were doing our jobs well and winning. They all said that we were spoiling rugby league as a spectacle, but if it meant more silverware for us, then we wanted to ruin it. Everyone wanted to beat us and be the ones that ended the run. But we were the only full-time professional team, and we knew that gave us a massive advantage. Everyone else eventually cottoned on, but we'd had two years head start, and that meant a lot.

That has to go down to Maurice Lindsay's foresight as well. It might not have been all his money, but you have to take your hat off to him for seeing what full time professionalism would mean for the club. Eventually St Helens, Leeds, Bradford and the rest reaped their own rewards from going full time, but they were never going to get there overnight. In the meantime, we had continued to set the standards so high that it took the others years and years to catch up.

EIGHTEEN

Down – But Not Out

The morning I awoke to realise I was no longer in charge of Salford left me with a very strange feeling. After all, it was the first day in 25 years when I was not involved in rugby league. Since the age of 12 or so I had always been preparing for a match as a player or coach. Mind you, I was in such a state at the time that I don't think it really hit home. Not a lot did, to be honest, because I wasn't really focused on anything.

When I called it a day as a player it never bothered me, and that is the God's honest truth. I know a lot of people who have never really got over their retirement, but I just accepted the fact, even though I could probably have gone on for another couple of years or so. Coaching, on the other hand, had really got me down. I remember when I told John Wilkinson that I had decided to pack it in, he was very genuine in wishing me the best of luck. John wanted me to get back to being the chirpy, bubbly Andy Greg who had first walked into the Willows, and at that time I was a million miles away from him. I am still not there, but I'm a hell of a lot closer than I was.

There are still days when I am very low, and you can hardly get a word out of me. And before anyone beats me to it, I know there will probably be plenty who are saying that it's not before time! The difference nowadays is that I accept it, whereas in the past I would have headed for the nearest bar to cheer myself up. Only the other week, for example, I was on a bit of a downer. I went to the Cheshire Show with Mike Nicholas and had a great day, but was still in a depressed mood. We were at one of the attractions when a group of mentally handicapped children came up asking for autographs and pictures. That made me realise how lucky I was – there was I feeling sorry for myself, yet all those youngsters had smiles a mile wide because they had met someone they'd seen on the TV.

Having said that, I look at sporting superstars such as Stan Collymore and Ronnie O'Sullivan booking into clinics to be treated for depression, and I do feel some sympathy for them because I know how it can affect you. I don't know if I will ever come out the other side as the same person, but I am giving it an almighty go. And I do feel proud of myself in a way, because I think that all I have been through over the last few years would have sent a lot of people over the edge. I am glad that I was strong enough within myself to get through.

One day I spoke to Roy Jackson and his wife Pam, who are both good mates of mine, and she gave me some great advice as well as a few phone numbers for people who might be able to help me out. I actually rang one organisation that deals in depression and drink, and made arrangements to go and see someone. But I am a firm believer that if you are going to sort yourself out, there is only one person who can do it. In my case, that person is Andy Gregory himself. I reckon I am doing an excellent job of it as well.

I have also had a lot of support from Alison, who I started seeing a couple of years ago, when I was at the lowest point of my life. I don't think she realised how low I was. She is just what I need – she's not a name-dropper, and she certainly isn't after me for my money, because I haven't got any! We just met and clicked, and she has been a massive help to me ever since.

There have obviously been a few others who have always been there for me as well. People like my brother Bryn and my mum – although at the moment I am in the doghouse with her, because she's just found out that I have had a tattoo. I had an English rose done, with 'Lauren' in the middle. I had had it for about four months before my mum spotted it and gave me hell.

Yet of all the advice I have ever received, the best that any individual gave me came when I was only a youngster, in the early days at St Pat's. And, needless to say, I ignored it. I never knew the guy's name, but he was an old man of about 80 who had watched the club for years. He called me over and said: 'Ee, Gregory, tha's the best player I have ever seen at this club – you'll have a great rugby league career, you'll be an international and everything.' I was only a kid, and I was absolutely made up – until he added: 'You'll have a million hangers-on, but when your career is over and your money's gone, you'll be able to count on the fingers of one hand who your friends are.' I really wish I had taken that advice, because if ever I've been given words of wisdom, those were the ones.

My biggest downfall over the years has been never being able to say no. If anyone ever wanted tickets for Manchester United, race meetings, pop concerts or Test matches, I would sort them out. At times I felt like a cross between Stan Flashman and Harvey Goldsmith. Whenever anyone asked me to open a garden fête or come to a dinner or whatever, I would agree. And now that they have drained me dry and spent my money, they have moved on to someone else. These days I know who my real friends are – and there aren't too many of them. If ever I can help any of them out in the future, I will do so without hesitation, because they have stood by me. Unfortunately for everyone else who asks, they might as well save their breath because the answer will be a very definite NO!

I wish someone had said that to me when it first crossed my mind about running a pub. My reckoning was that I was spending so much time in the pub that I might as well go and get one of my own. In hindsight it was a massive mistake, but at the time I had nowhere else to go. The scrap business had gone with my divorce, which was a pity because I had enjoyed that and my time working in the demolition game with Sammy Evans. The funny thing was that when I first got the Bluebell at Newton-le-Willows, and later the Clubhouse, near the JJB Stadium, I had no desire to have a drink in either. And since I came back from Spain, I can assure you that I will never, ever again take over a pub like I did in the past.

I actually took over the Bluebell on the day before Salford played Sheffield in that infamous 1998 Challenge Cup semi-final. A friend of mine had advised me not to go into the business, but by that stage no one could speak to me. Everything that anyone said fell on deaf ears. After a while I got the chance to run the Clubhouse, near the new Wigan ground. The brewery knew of my interest in both football and, obviously, rugby league, and I thought it was a great prospect, even though the pub had a reputation as being a bit of a rough house. When I first went in, most of my time was spent getting rid of potential troublemakers and trying to clean it up. But after a while I just lost interest in it, because I was fighting a losing battle. I thought the best thing in the long run was to tell the brewery and move on – contrary to reports that will eventually be proved wrong in court, which suggested I just did a runner.

Most days at the Clubhouse were monotonously the same. I'd get up, the same old faces would come in, there would be a few drinks, and that would be it. It's a pity, because that place could be a good pub, but it just wasn't for me. Nothing anyone said or did at that time could lift me out of my slump. I knew that people in the pub were shafting me over drinks and money going missing out of the till, but I simply wasn't bothered any more. To be honest, there wasn't a lot in life in general that I could be bothered with. I was being ripped off all over the place, but I had had enough of everything.

There were times when it was like playing again, when I had to put my body on the line, because it wasn't a particularly nice place. I tried to improve it, but I was banging my head against a brick wall. Some people don't have any respect for anything or anyone. If they broke a window or a glass, or put a dent in the wall, then what the hell – as far as they were concerned, it was normal and acceptable behaviour. I wouldn't dream of going into someone's home and acting like some of those people did in mine. You wouldn't go into another person's house and not give a toss if you ruined it.

There was one incident in particular which brought things to a head. One night there was loads of trouble and a huge fight, which ended with the police being called. It all started between a couple of lads, but it blew up to such extent that about 12 police vans arrived. A mate of mine drove past and saw all this, and said to me the next day, 'What the hell are you doing in a place like that – do you honestly need all that crap?' Amazingly – because, as I said, not too many people could get through to me then – it brought me to my senses, and I realised that there was more to life than standing behind a bar or propping one up on the other side. That's when I decided to get out and had a word with the brewery. And, touch wood, so far I haven't looked back, although it has been bloody hard at times.

Four weeks before I eventually left I met the area manager. I told him the date when I was leaving, but I asked him if he would keep it as quiet as possible because I didn't want any leaving parties or a big send-off. I just wanted to get out as quickly as possible, without any fuss. On the Monday morning when it was time to go I met him again, and another couple of people about the fixtures and fittings. I also met the new landlord who was coming in from the pub support company to replace me, and I spent two and a half hours showing him around the place. We went around everything – the living quarters, the bar, the cellar, which key fitted which lock, the lot. Eventually I left at around lunchtime, went to the Lord Daresbury Hotel just outside Warrington, and the next day I flew out to Spain. Only a few people knew I was going – obviously my mum, Bryn and Dawn. On the Sunday before I went, I was the summariser on the radio commentary team for the Salford–Warrington Cup tie on BBC GMR. Trevor Hunt, the commentator, asked me where they should send the cheque, and I told him I was going away for a few months, and I'd get him an address. I wanted to go with as little to-do as possible.

It was vital for me to get out. I was in financial trouble, and my health was suffering too. In fact, it had got so bad that I firmly believe if I had stayed in the pub game and carried on living as I was, then I wouldn't have been alive for much longer. I was looking straight through the people who genuinely wanted to help, and listening to the hangers-on. I remember some so-called friends, who knew I was struggling with drink and depression, coming over to one of the pubs to help me. At least, that's what they said. When they arrived they took me straight to another pub down the road and bought me eight large Jack Daniels and Coke, while they downed a few themselves as well. I thought they were mates who had my best interests at heart, but all they had come over for was a day on the drink with me.

A lot of people have said and still say, 'Greg's a belting bloke, he's always got a smile on his face' – and that was definitely true at one stage. I would go anywhere to have a laugh and a joke. I didn't set out to be the centre of attention. But, without wishing to sound big-headed, I have a good sense of humour, I'm quick-witted, and I suppose I was good company to knock about with. Unfortunately, I didn't realise that some people – whatever mess I was in with my personal life – still only saw me like that.

Not that I realised. I would open the pub at eleven o'clock with no intention of having a drink. But when the first customers arrived they'd buy me one, so I felt duty bound to buy them one back. They'd get me another, and I'd buy another back. By the time they left I would have had four pints – and then the lunchtime crew would come in, and the same would happen. At five o'clock the tea-time shift would arrive, and by the time it was eight or so, I'd be fast asleep, blind drunk. I know people will say that I should have refused the first one, but that is easier said than done. Especially in the state I was in at the time. And don't forget, the people who were buying me booze were supposedly my friends. They'd want me to tell them about Wembley, or a story from a Great Britain tour, and there were times when I enjoyed it because in my warped frame of mind I thought it was okay to live like that.

Nowadays I know differently. Although there are days when I am down, a lot of the time I feel smashing. Everyone knows that I was a choirboy when I was a youngster, and I have been to church regularly since I got back to England. Every Sunday at 11.30 a.m. I have a cup of coffee and a chat with the rest of the congregation after the service, and they are all absolutely made up to see me doing well. They are all genuine people who know that I've had a bit of fame and loads of pats in the back, and who know that I've been taken for a ride as a result. People like Derek and Irene Stott from the Fourth Wigan Cub Scouts. As a kid I went on camps with them, and even now whenever they see my mum, they always ask, 'How's Andrew?' Like the bloke said at Pat's, 'You'll have a million acquaintances and very few friends.' Derek and Irene are certainly friends.

Another really good mate of mine was a guy called John Harper, who ran the Bees Knees and the Wiganer pubs. He was a pal for 20 years, and it broke my heart when they buried him recently. I went to see his wife Gill after he died, and there were a lot of genuine tears from the pair of us. One of the best nights I ever had was after Wigan had beaten Manly in the 1987 World Club Challenge, and we all went back to the Bees Knees. John was an absolute rugby league nut, and his pub was full of memorabilia. He was a really close mate of Steve Hampson, too, but I think if you'd asked him who his favourite player was, it would have been a toss-up between me and Henderson Gill. You could tell how popular he was from the amazing number of people who went to his funeral. I and plenty of others will be doing our best to help Gill get over it.

That sort of thing puts everything in perspective. I remember the first real experience I had of someone close to me passing away. One bloke I really looked up to as a kid was my uncle, Eric Ayles, and I still remember that it was a Thursday when he died. I came home from school, and my mum said that he had been killed, but it didn't really sink in for a while. For some reason it only hit me when I went to choir practice that night. He actually got killed building the new stand at Central Park; he had a big dump truck, and a huge concrete plinth fell on to his cab. He was one hell of a nice man, and he would have loved to see how my career progressed. He had played for Belle Vue Rangers, but he was a Wigan director, and he would have been made up to see me doing well for the club. That sort of thing really does put everything into perspective.

Another example of the same thing came when I was living in Newton-le-Willows. I was feeling particularly sorry for myself one day towards the end of my playing career. I was sitting in the Blue Lion pub, looking out of the window and thinking how bad a time I was having of it all. I walked out and crossed the road with my head down, and the first thing I saw when I looked up was one of the Sunshine coaches, full of underprivileged kids. I suddenly thought, 'What's wrong with you, Gregory? You've had a great career, you've got a few quid and you've got your health.'

In those days I thought that if I had a drink, it would make me feel better, but all it did was make me feel worse. I had nothing physically wrong with me, I had money in my pocket, and I was fit and well – really, there wasn't a lot to be down in the mouth about. Whenever I get low these days, I try to remember things like that. That's why I try to raise money for my local church and the like. I also want to help out kids in the game and teach them how to handle pressure. Rugby league can be a great life, but you have to take care of yourself. I wish I had.

If I talk to youngsters now, I always tell them to keep an eye out for the hangers-on. I don't worry so much about how much they drink, but I know from experience that there are some idiots around who think it is funny to spike your drinks, and that can cost lives. I want to educate youngsters about that, and help the kids who are setting out in the game with things like handling the media and dealing with life in the spotlight.

If you are suddenly thrown in at the deep end, you can find

yourself in all sorts of trouble. I remember the first tour I made of Australia in 1984. Their media were rubbishing us before the plane had even touched down. As soon as we arrived we had a press conference and they were firing loads of questions at me. I had no idea how to handle it, and I think I must have set a record for the number of times I said 'you know' in the interview. I think 47 was the final count. They promptly edited it so that those two words were all that were left of what I had said, so that they could just take the mickey out of me.

While I admit that I have had a good life out of rugby league, I also think that I have put plenty back into it. When I left Salford and went into the pub game, I honestly believed that my involvement with the game had ended for good – but in hindsight, that break from it all probably saved my life. I always used to put a brave face on things and try to have a joke, but people never knew how bad a time I was having. These days it is great to be able to go over to the Daresbury Park Hotel, or the Russian baths at Wigan International Pool; you'd be surprised how many rugby league experts go there. I see Alex Murphy there quite a lot, and we generally put the world to rights – we call it the 'Think Tank'. It is so refreshing to come out of there and feel healthy, rather than walking round with a banging headache.

Yet you should know by now that nothing ever seems to go as smoothly as planned for me. And that little excursion to Spain was no different. Not by a long chalk . . .

NINETEEN

Friend or Foe

I set a few records during my career, but one of the more offbeat ones must have been as the man who had more best friends than anyone else. I couldn't tell you how many people asked me for favours over the years, whether it was tickets for Manchester United, hospitality at Lancashire or England cricket matches, or getting them in at Central Park. And every time, like an idiot, I said yes. What made it even crazier was that half the time it actually used to cost me money to get people into these places. Over the years, Dawn, and now Alison, have told me countless times that I am too soft, but it has only been throughout the past few months that I have realised they were right.

There used to be a saying that it's not far from the penthouse to the shithouse, and if ever anything was true, it's that. When I was spending time in the penthouse, everyone wanted a piece of me. As soon as I got close to the other place, apparently I wasn't even worth a phone call. And by that I don't just mean the

hangers-on, but blokes I rated as really good friends. To say they have disappointed me is the understatement of all time. The way people turned their back on me did surprise me, but it also highlighted the truth of what that old guy told me in the early days at St Pat's.

During my days at Wigan there were certain superstars in the side who would never do interviews, and were very reluctant to present trophies or to conduct coaching clinics for kids. It always seemed to be Andy Gregory, Shaun Wane and Joe Lydon who ended up going along. Half the time that was fair enough, although on more than one occasion it would cost us money to do so. That was not the issue as far as I was concerned – but what did rankle with me a little was the fact that I never seemed to get a vote of thanks from the club for helping out.

You could virtually guarantee that after every training session on a Tuesday or Thursday night, I would end up going along to some amateur club or other. Now I didnt necessarily mind that, but I do think there should have been some instructions from the management to set up a rota system whereby everyone had to take their turn. But because Andy Gregory was the player in the limelight, Andy Gregory was always the player they wanted to go. I could never say no, and I think they played on that as well.

Now the same people who were always asking me for favours are the ones who are intent on spreading gossip or having a dig at every opportunity. I just feel sorry for the next sporting superstar that the leeches get stuck into. I helped out everyone, from high-class businessmen to Joe Public, but if I'd had to rely on them in return over the past few months I would really be in trouble.

I used to be in Wigan's Past Players Association, and I put a lot of time and effort into helping them over the years with things like dinners and testimonials. In fact, three years after I retired I played in one myself, for Gary Chambers and Chris Rudd, while I have also played at the JJB Stadium for the Wigan Legends team against the youngsters. But since I have been back from Spain, to tell you the truth, I haven't really been out much – despite what others will no doubt tell you – so I have lost touch with everyone a little.

Only recently I was watching a television programme on Diego Maradona. Now I am not for one minute suggesting that I am in the same league as him, but it highlighted again how people latch on to you when you are famous. For example, is Five Bellies really Gazzas best mate? And how many people jumped on to the George Best gravy train over the years?

To a lesser extent, that is exactly what happened to me, and in a small place like Wigan the rumours obviously go around a hell of a lot quicker. Now I don't claim to be a saint, not by any means. But a lot of people have marriage problems, a lot of people have financial trouble, and a lot of people have drink problems. One thing I could never be accused of is being a troublemaker, and I have never seriously gone out of my way to hurt anyone – but that hasn't stopped the stories. I have already told you how I was supposed to be a drug runner, yet I have never even touched a cigarette in my life. And I would need half a dozen twins if I was to have visited half the pubs and clubs that people have said they saw me in. That sort of thing doesn't necessarily wear me down, but there are times when I do wish that people would leave me alone.

The real mates I have now are the ones who see me in the pub with a soft drink, give me the thumbs-up, and tell me: 'You're doing great, Greg, stick at it.' I certainly don't need idiots like the one I had the other night. I was sitting with Alison sipping half a lime and soda when he came up, pointed at my glass and started making suggestions as to what I was really drinking. I just said I'm not bothered about what's in your glass, so don't start having a go at what's in mine.

It might seem a bit rich to hit back now, because I know I have upset people myself in the past, and I have let certain others down. Now as much as I might want to, there is nothing I can do to take that back, even though I bitterly regret it now that I am sober. But the way I see it is that, throughout my career both on and off the field, I pleased a lot more than I disappointed, and no one can take that away from me.

Not that everyone has proved a big disappointment and turned their back on me. I know I had my run-ins with John Wilkinson at Salford, but he has been an absolutely belting friend. So too has Phil Clarke, my old team-mate from Wigan, while Neil Midgley has also helped me out no end, as have Neil Hilton and Howard Clegg, of Salford, and my big mate Tommy Dickens. I like to see this as a chance to express a public vote of thanks to them. And to the lads from the Daresbury Park Hotel, like Mike Nicholas and especially Richard Gray. Trevor Lloyd and Roy Jackson deserve a huge pat on the back, while Steve McCormack and Mark Lee have always been there, as have the people from St Mary's Church.

From the early days there is obviously Cliff Fleming and Billy Atherton from St Pat's, as well as Frank O'Leary and Dave Pendlebury. Going back even earlier there was my old school pal Philip Ratcliff: I used to walk to school with Philip, and then he'd carry my bags and homework home when I stayed on – as I did most nights – for some sport or another. Then there's Bob and May Talbot, whose caravan in the Lake District we used to stay in a couple of times a year. Even people from my time with the Fourth Wigan Cub Scouts – folk like Derek and Irene Stott, along with their son Alan, who have kept the movement going, and Brian Phillips and Brian Holland. Of course there is also

Mavis Seels, the lady who got me the job at GUS all those years ago, along with her husband Jimmy. Then there's Fraser Boone, Barbara Wilcox, the old cub leader Bernie – or Stephen Tomkinson, to give him his real name – and, obviously, Alison. Those are just the ones I have remembered. If there are others that I have missed out, I can only apologise, because it has been a complete oversight.

Talking of the scouts, I still remember camping with them by Lake Windermere on one occasion when it was my birthday. A lot of the others had gone off on a ferry, but being interested in cookery I stayed back and decided to surprise them with a spot of baking. Together with a couple of others, I ended up paddling out to meet the ferry, carrying a tin of fairy cakes. Perhaps that's where it started going wrong for me: cooking, choirboys, scouts, cutting old ladies' hair – maybe I chose the wrong vocation. Mind you, each Christmas I also used to help out at Morgan's off-licence, carrying bottles and boxes up from the cellar. Perhaps that was more an omen of what was to come!

Of course, there are the two people who have always been there for me: my mum, Lois (even on occasions when we aren't talking!) and my brother, Bryn. It is people such as these who help me keep my spirits up. It's because of people like these, who have helped me out and stood by me, that I want to put something back in. For example, as I said earlier, I would love to work with the youth of rugby league. It would give me great pleasure to help kids work their way up through the ranks, and I would love to get into the schools and help them with their coaching.

I now know from the support of all these wonderful people that it's difficult to do it all on your own. On 8 August 2000, I gave a positive demonstration of that realisation: for the first time in my life, I registered with a GP. I have never actually had a doctor since the days when I first started playing, largely because I always felt okay. On the few occasions when I might have needed medical attention, there was always the guy from whichever club I was with at the time. Chris Brooks at Salford was especially good, while Doc Zaman at Wigan was known as 'Gis-a-Jab' because of all the injections he gave – although nine times out of ten he would have me back to fighting fitness before I knew it. I decided to take the plunge in early August because I hadn't been feeling too clever for a while, and I was quickly diagnosed as being asthmatic. I had the blood tests and the X-rays, and was as surprised as anyone when they gave me an inhaler.

Maybe in hindsight I could have done with a bit more professional help when I was suffering from depression. The thing about that is that, when it gets you, nothing else matters. You can talk about financial trouble, and I have had as much as anyone recently, but things like bills and suchlike just don't seem to compare. On the subject of money, people from bank managers to accountants have told me countless times in the past that I should have someone to manage my affairs, and if I had no doubt I would be a very wealthy man by now. But you can't turn the clock back, and I have just got to make the best of it from here on in. As Oasis sang, 'Don't Look Back In Anger'. Or, as far as Andy Gregory is concerned, perhaps Monty Python would be more appropriate, because I plan to 'Always Look On the Bright Side of Life'.

What I found particularly pleasing was a day out I enjoyed at Old Trafford recently, when I went to the Friday of the England-West Indies Test match as a guest of the Lancashire groundsman, my good pal Peter Marron. We enjoyed all the usual hospitality and had a couple of drinks – literally a couple, not a dozen – and then we headed for home at the close of play. But whereas in the past that would have been followed by a full Saturday and Sunday on the booze, with quite possibly Monday and Tuesday thrown in as well, this time it was different. On Saturday morning I was up and about early to go for a walk, followed by an afternoon sitting in front of the television watching the cricket again. That was something I could never have managed in the past.

Then on the Sunday I was up at 4.30 a.m. with my brother Bryn and my mate Mark to head down to Brands Hatch on the motorbikes. I was only riding pillion, so they were the ones who really suffered with a five-and-a-half-hour journey each way. We had another great day with all the hospitality, this time thanks to Trevor Lloyd, and apart from the guy who ended up winning the Superbikes, I think Bryn had the biggest smile in the place. There have been countless times in the past when I have been to sporting events and really gone to town on the free food and free bar. This time, though, I hadn't had a single drink, and I think that really left its mark on my brother. After all, he has seen me on plenty of occasions when I would struggle to get in the back of a car, let alone on the back of a bike.

I personally realised then that things were on the up and up. I am a little shamefaced to admit it, but up until the age of 38 I had never watched a television soap opera in my life. My own existence was probably the closest I got to it, but I have started watching them now. That alone is a good indication of how things are changing. In the past I was never able to sit down and listen to music or watch the box. The first opportunity I got, I would be out of the door and down to the nearest bar. Over the past few months, though, I have grown up a hell of a lot – if you consider turning into a big *Coronation Street* fan growing up.

I'm also becoming into something of a film buff. I have never been the best sleeper in the world, but because of the incredible turnaround in my life, I have found it even more difficult to drop off recently. And so it has got to the point where I have been watching three videos a night. Last night I saw Sylvester Stallone in *The Assassin* and *Cliffhanger*, followed by Tom Hanks in *Saving Private Ryan*. Maybe they'll end up making a film of my life – although, with all the mistakes I've made, they'll probably settle for a remake of *Dumb and Dumber*!

TWENTY

The Brawl Boys

Warrington and Wigan produced some fantastic matches during my time as a player. They also left the players on both sides with more bruises than they'd collect from the rest of the season. As with any local derby, things quite often got a little out of hand– and never more so than one New Year's Day showdown. It would have been more appropriate had it taken place on Boxing Day. In fact it would have been more appropriate if it had been staged at Madison Square Garden.

The rivalry between the clubs in the late 1980s was as fierce as it had been for some time, and this one match at Wilderspool was no exception. The biggest surprise was that a rugby match occasionally broke out and interrupted the violence! I remember I was standing in front of the posts at the Warrington end when Andy Goodway got sent off for flattening Paul Cullen. There was never any love lost between those two, and they could both handle themselves, so all the ingredients were there. As Andy walked off he made a slight detour and managed to tread all over Cull's hand. It was quite appropriate that this was a Christmas game, because what happened next was right out of the pantomime season. Goodway carried on going, and Cull jumped to his feet, chased after him and belted him. Just before he made contact, everyone on the Wigan bench jumped up. It was just like something you see at the Palace Theatre – the whole lot of them shouting, 'Behind you, behind you,' just before Paul whacked him. I don't think Cull ever saw his red card because, before the referee had time to send him off, Warrington coach Tony Barrow jumped up and threw him straight down the tunnel. Unforgettable!

The weirdest place Wigan ever played Warrington was in the Milwaukee Brewers Stadium in 1989, as part of a drive to get rugby league up and running in America. I flew in from Australia, where I was guesting for Illawarra, and so did Steve Hampson, Joe Lydon, Ellery Hanley and Shaun Edwards, who were all with various clubs Down Under. The preparation for the game certainly beat running around Wigan on a freezing winter morning, as we headed for a magnificent man-made beach in the scorching heat. The only problem was the pitch itself. The Milwaukee Brewers were a baseball team, and the pitcher's mound was bang in the middle. The Americans had also cut 25 yards off the width, making it the smallest pitch I'd played on since I was about eight.

It was hardly the setting for free-flowing, expansive rugby, and the game couldn't be described as a classic. There was only one try, when I put Andy Goodway through a gap, but at least we emerged with a win. The most memorable thing was the sledging that went on, which in itself was nothing new – but because the pitch was so small, you could hear every word wherever you were. For 80 minutes all I heard was Les Boyd and

Ellery Hanley trading insults. Having said that, I can't ever remember any on-field disputes being taken into the player's bar afterwards, which is probably true of all sporting rivalries. If someone copped you in the game, you just accepted it and learned to look after yourself, and the American challenge match was no different. The day after the game both teams met up on the beach with boxes of iced beer and we generally had a great time.

That wasn't quite so true for a gang of British lads living over there who challenged us to a game of rugby league. We agreed, on the basis that it was only a friendly contest for a laugh – but we did warn them not to run straight at Des Drummond. Whether they didn't realise that we were being serious, or they thought that they were tougher than they actually were, I still don't know. But during the game one of them put his head down and made a beeline for Des. Now Dessie was a really hard so-and-so, as countless opponents over the years will testify. He rarely missed when he lined up a shot, and I can assure you that this was no exception: he put the lad straight on his backside and knocked him clean out. There weren't many others on their team who were too keen to run at him after that.

Des was also at the centre of one of the most amusing things I ever saw on a rugby pitch. He was playing for Leigh at the time, and my Widnes team were due to play them at Hilton Park. We were being refereed by an Aussie who obviously hadn't seen snow before, because it was bucketing down and we were amazed when he decided that the game should go ahead. In fact, ours was the only match to be played that weekend, the weather was that bad.

It was a complete nightmare, it never stopped snowing all afternoon and all 26 players were absolutely freezing. During the match I looked over to the touch-line, where Des was playing on the wing, and I couldn't stop myself from laughing out loud. There he was, this forlorn coloured winger, doing his best to keep warm. All the snow had settled on his head, and he looked just like a pint of Guinness.

It was so cold that day that even my mum, who has never been one for drinking, bought me a large whisky in the clubhouse after the game to try to warm me up. It was just as cold when I made my Salford début at Hull KR. It was so bad that one of our players, Chris Tauro, actually went off with hypothermia. When the game finished we all rushed into the dressing-room and he was still standing under a hot shower, flanked by the doctor and the kitman, with his full kit on.

One of the funniest scraps took place during my early days with Widnes, when we travelled to play Featherstone Rovers. One of the scrums erupted when Steve O'Neill and Steve Hankins started fighting, and both got their marching orders. In those days Featherstone used to have a walkway under the stand on the way to the tunnel, and as the pair of them were walking off, miles from play, we heard the crowd roaring as they carried on their disagreement *en route* to the dressing-room. After the game I asked Steve O'Neill what had gone on, and he said, 'Hankins kept mouthing off at me, so I turned round and bit him on the ear.' Half an hour later Hankins appeared in the players' bar with a big turban on his head, looking just like a Sikh. Steve came up to me and said, 'I was going to ask him if he fancied a pint, but he'd only tell me he's got one ear!'

I got stitched plenty of times over the years, although one time when it didn't come courtesy of the club doctor was also at Featherstone. It was only about my sixth game for Widnes, and I was Man of the Match as we beat the Rovers in the quarter-final of the Challenge Cup. In the players' lounge after the match the team made sure that I was sitting at the end of a table, near the stage. I thought nothing of it, because I assumed that was to make it easier for me to get out when they made the Man of the Match presentation. Ten minutes later, three strippers came on and – as the rest of the lads had instructed – made a beeline straight for me. There was I, a baby-faced innocent, faced with the prospect of being hauled on stage in front of everyone. I wasn't having any of that, and I put everybody else's drinks in front of me so they couldn't get hold of me. It turned out to be the best Man of the Match award I ever got in my life!

As playmaker for the various teams I represented during my career, I would go on to the field knowing that I was the man the opposition wanted to put out of action – and that did toughen me up. Mick Adams used to point me in the right direction when I first started at Widnes, and I also picked up a lot of good advice by listening to other people's conversations, which helped me a lot. But there were always going to be occasions when I couldn't avoid trouble, like the first game I played on the 1984 Lions tour, in Wagga Wagga. I had the ball and was held up in the tackle, unable to get a pass out, and desperately trying to wriggle my way away from the two defenders. The opposition scrum-half obviously thought it was too good a chance to miss, because he came in with a flying head butt that caught me above the eye and needed 16 stitches.

Another time I ended up with the needle came during my Leeds career, when we were playing Bradford. David Hobbs caught me off the ball with a really good one that required another dozen stitches to the eye. It was quite deliberate, but you knew you were playing a tough game, and you just accepted that things like that would happen from time to time.

In my early career, I used to enjoy my battles with Kevin Dick of Leeds, and when it was nip and tuck between Wigan and Widnes for the mantle of the top team in the game, I had some unbelievable contests with David Hulme. They usually ended with referee Colin Morris sending me off! Hulme, who I went on to coach at Salford, ranks alongside Ellery Hanley as the most determined player I've ever come across. David would be the first to hold his hands up and admit that he wasn't the most talented man ever to play the game. He didn't have the skills to be rated among the best half-backs in the world, and he lacked the physical presence to be a top-level back-row forward – but his will to win more than made up for his deficiencies. If his physique had been as big as his heart, he would have gone down as one of the all-time greats.

While he was tough, David would never go down in anyone's book as the best fighter in the world. Someone who would be a contender for that particular award is Kevin Tamati, the old Widnes and Warrington front-row forward, who was responsible for one of the best scraps I ever saw, when he knocked seven bells out of Australia's Greg Dowling in a Test match for New Zealand at Lang Park. Kevin had a few problems when he first played in England, but he stuck it out and fully deserved all the rewards he went on to get. When he was hooker between Les Boyd and Bob Jackson at Warrington, it was one of the most fearsome front rows the club has ever had. You certainly wouldn't mess about with them. I remember one game for Widnes at Bradford, when I got my marching orders: I was back in the dressing-room when the door flew open, and Kevin and Eric Prescott both came in in quick succession. We had three men sent off, but we should still have won that game.

At that time at Odsal, you used to have to walk up a track to get off the pitch. There wasn't a tunnel as such, just that track, which was always covered in mud and crap. All the Bradford fans used to gather round it and give you loads of stick. They were even above you, so there was no way of avoiding them – which led to an unforgettable incident in one Challenge Cup tie. Tony

Myler had one of his best games for us, but the Widnes hero was his brother John, who dropped a goal in the last minute to win it. At the end of the game, as we came off the field, the Bradford fans were really giving us bucketloads of abuse. I'd actually had quite a quiet game, but that apparently made no difference to one particular idiot. As I approached he took a huge swing at me, but I saw it coming and ducked. The kitman, immediately behind me, wasn't quite as fortunate and took the blow full in the face. I carried on going and was followed into the dressing-room by a kitman carrying two buckets, and sporting a bloody nose.

Someone who was always more than willing to give it a go was Les Davidson, who I was lucky enough to play with at Warrington. I remember watching one game he played in, when I was on the terraces at Widnes, and he took on the home pack single-handed at Naughton Park. They had some great names in the forwards at the time – people such as Kurt Sorensen and Emosi Koloto, and they were all big lads. Les wasn't doing anything underhand, but he just took them all on one by one – and he came out on top as well.

Another lad who could look after himself was a guy called Carl Webb, who I had played against many times at amateur level before he went on to Warrington. When I was a youngster at Widnes, he caught me with a belter bang on the chin. We both knew it was a good one, and he was expecting me to go down. But I was determined to stay on my feet, and I even managed to ask him, 'Is that your best shot?' If it wasn't, I'd have hated him to get me with the one that was! Alan Rathbone was another Warrington player who had a fearsome reputation – although I think as much as anything that it was something that just accumulated and then stuck with him throughout his career. Of course he could handle himself, but he certainly wasn't as bad as people made him out to be. And it undermined his image a little when I read in the *Warrington Guardian* about his hobby of rearing exotic cats.

One of the nastiest injuries I ever received was self-inflicted. It came during my days with Wigan, in a game against Halifax, when I caught Karl Harrison on the head with an attempted tackle – God knows how I got that high. My hand was immediately killing me, and I looked down to see the bone sticking out of my finger. I was screaming at physio Keith Mills to come on and treat it, but as soon as he saw my hand he said, 'Oh God, Greg, don't show me that,' and looked away. And this was the bloke who was supposed to be putting it right! I think I might sue the Rugby Football League for that one, because I've always wanted to be a piano player, and that put paid to that!

I got in the ambulance to go to hospital, still in my kit and boots, and all covered in mud. Wigan chairman Maurice Lindsay came with me, and the doctor bandaged my finger and sorted me out. But when I came out of the treatment room I found that Maurice had gone back to watch the game – so I had to run all the way back to Central Park from Wigan Infirmary, still in my kit. By this time the crowd were leaving the ground as the match had finished – and there was I, running past them all down Wigan Lane to get back to the stadium!

If you asked anyone who is the toughest player they know, I think nine out of ten would give you the same answer – themselves. You have to have not only confidence in your own ability, but also the belief that you can look after yourself. I always thought I was the toughest because I was the smallest bloke on the field, yet I managed to cope against all these bigger guys who were invariably trying to knock me out of the game. It's not being big-headed, it is just having self-belief – and I think virtually everyone who has ever played rugby league would make the same comment about himself.

TWENTY-ONE

There are Places I Remember

It isn't only in recent seasons that the Rugby Football League has come under fire for its efforts to take the game to new areas. One of the stranger decisions came in my early international career, when some bright spark insisted that Italy was a country ripe for the introduction of the sport. After various talks, an exhibition match was arranged as part of a joint venture between Great Britain and France.

So midway through the season we all headed off to Venice for five days. As a spectacle designed to get the Italians interested in rugby league, it was something of a disaster. Matches between the French and us were rarely classics around that time, and this was another great experience of my run-ins with them. We ended up losing narrowly, for what it meant, and the little stadium just outside the city was hardly packed to capacity. The game also went out live on television, but I never heard anything about viewing figures breaking any records. But for the rest of the trip we had a ball, taking in all the sights and generally having a good time. We went out on the gondolas, and that was my overriding memory of the visit – all that bloody water. At least I had the benefit of being a decent swimmer if anything went wrong! And as for the Italian venture – I can only assume they didn't show any interest in taking it further because we never went back.

That was just one example of how rugby league took us to places that otherwise we could only have dreamed of. There was also that memorable trip to Milwaukee – but we were always going to be up against it trying to crack that particular market. Some of the forwards in our team didn't know all the rules, so what chance did the Yanks have?

My mum actually came out on that trip to America, as did plenty of other Wigan and Warrington fans. I'm just grateful she wasn't staying in the same hotel as us, or else she would have got the shock of her life when, after the game, we stripped Graham Lowe naked and threw him out of the lift into the reception. In hindsight, maybe it's no big surprise that the Americans were more than a little wary of our game!

TWENTY-TWO

Ref Justice

I don't think the name Andy Gregory would appear on the Christmas card lists of too many referees, but I honestly never felt that I had that much of a problem with them. At least, I didn't once the game itself had finished. Colin Morris, Steve Ganson, the two Connollys . . . I have had my run-ins with all of them over the years, but I cannot ever remember taking any incident into the bar after the match.

One thing that does annoy me is the way refs seem to perceive themselves nowadays. In my playing career I really used to admire men like Billy Thompson, Mick Naughton, Fred Lindop and Ronnie Campbell. These days, though, with the advent of the big screen and all the TV coverage, the refs seem to want to become as big as the players. Billy would have laughed his socks off at the mere suggestion of his receiving a fan letter – but these days it seems to be the norm, certainly in Australia.

These days the refs look stressed out before they even get on the field. I know there is a lot of pressure on them, because everything they do is scrutinised through video replays, and there is so much more money at stake. It is one job you would never, ever catch me doing. Having said that, though, they do get paid for it – and no one held a gun to their head and forced them to become a referee.

The one incident that everyone seems to remember with me – as a coach, at least – is when I let Steve Ganson know exactly what I thought of him during one televised game against Sheffield. He had given a decision against us – I think he penalised Peter Edwards for something at the play-the-ball – and I called him a fat St Helens so-and-so. Unfortunately the Sky cameras and microphones picked it all up, and I was up in front of the Rugby Football League before you knew it. Funnily enough, Steve is a big friend of mine – but I still think he got it wrong. We actually had a drink together after the match, although at that time I don't think he knew what I had called him. That outburst cost me £1,500, and I'm convinced it was only so severe because it was me. Only recently we saw someone make a one-finger gesture as she came off the Centre Court at Wimbledon in front of millions on BBC Television, and she only got fined £750. If that had been me, they would have locked me up and thrown away the key!

I had a further run-in with Steve after another game, and this time he showed his funny side. I was always telling him that he wasn't fit enough, and how the refs were all part-timers in a full-time game. I'd obviously told him this one too many times, because he turned around to me and said, 'Greg, I'll race you or any of your players – apart from the wingers – over 100 metres, and I will beat them all.' I just had to admit to him that, fair enough, we didn't have the fastest team in the league.

Steve came with us when Salford played a Super League game in France against Paris. Before the game, obviously, we kept away from each other, but afterwards I invited him to join us for a few drinks and a game of cards back at the hotel. There aren't too many officials I would have done that with – although if I'd realised we would be up until nearly three o'clock in the morning while he won all our money, I might have had second thoughts!

But I reached the stage where I couldn't even pass a light-hearted comment about referees without being in trouble. I remember one Sunday morning when I went down to Wigan St Jude's to watch an amateur game, and I bumped into the Connolly brothers, John and Bob. I couldn't stop laughing from the moment I saw them. When we were youngsters, my mum used to get Bryn and me dressed up in our finest clothes for Wigan Walking Day – the typical stuff, both of us wearing exactly the same. Anyway, the Connollys both turned up looking exactly like that in their replica Super League shirts and the rest of the gear – they probably even had official underpants on! We all knew they were bloody twins, without them having to sport identical clothes as well. It was around that time I said that if the Connollys were made of chocolate, they would eat themselves. Cue for another slap on the wrists from the Rugby Football League.

I made a few comments about one referee after an Alliance team game, when one of the Salford lads had been knocked out and the incident had gone unpunished. Even though I was shouting the odds about him from inside my own changing-room, someone obviously heard me from the outside, because I was in trouble for that as well. I could have taken all the punishments and warnings from the League if I had felt that the same rules applied to everyone. But how many times have you seen players or coaches cursing officials when a decision has gone against them? Invariably nothing happens to them, but as soon as it's Andy Gregory the League gets all heavy-handed. I know I didn't help my cause by not exactly being a yes-man to the hierarchy, and because of that they probably classed me as trouble. But that was unfair in my book. Apparently it was okay for some coaches to bag officials, but not for me to do the same.

Some coaches seemed to spend a hell of a lot of time meeting and talking with Greg McCallum, the League's controller of referees, while certain others never sat down in his office to discuss things. I was one of the latter. Perhaps I have got it wrong, but it seemed to me that the ones who were in there a lot appeared to get the right decisions the following weekend. Having said that, Greg remains the best referee that I ever played under. He has controlled Test matches between Great Britain and Australia, which were always likely to explode at any time, and he always did so better than anyone else. He's certainly the best ref that I ever told to f*** off!

Which brings me on to another point about modern-day officials – the lack of communication. Years ago you used to be able to talk to the refs a heck of a lot more. The banter with them was just part of the game. Of course, you used to know who you could push further than others, but the give-and-take seemed to be accepted a lot more. Nowadays you face being penalised as soon as you open your mouth to half of the refs. As I came to the end of my career, it seemed that I only had to look at them and a penalty was awarded against me.

At some stage of a game you knew that if someone gave you a good, hard tackle – and I don't necessarily mean a dirty one or a cheap shot – you would be able to give them one back later on. I remember someone once catching me with a beauty at Hull KR – I think it was Roy Holdstock. Nothing was said, but I had his card marked. In the second half the chance arrived to cop him back with an absolute belter, which I duly did. As I went back into the defensive line Stan Wall, the referee, looked at me and said, 'It's 1–1 now, Andy, let's leave it at that.' And that's just the way it was. There was no need for discussions with either of us, or to refer the incident to someone at the Rugby Football League to consider over endless video replays. And it didn't necessarily mean that people went round trying it on a lot more either.

I believe that, these days, a lot of referees take the soft option and cop out of making a decision because they can put a player on report. I know a lot more is picked up on television now, and while I am in favour of the big screen in some ways, there are a lot of others that do annoy me. In theory it is a great idea, but it does lead to a lack of consistency – not in the use of the screen itself, but in the fact that it is only ever present at one or two games per weekend. I know it is a question of finance, but if we are going to have it, then it should be at every match. A try could be awarded in a match with a three o'clock kick-off with no TV coverage that would be disallowed if it took place at 7.30 p.m., purely because the referee would refer it to the fourth official. If the big screen leads to the right decision being made, then I am all for it – but how can it be fair when the same rules don't apply to each game? It all comes down to consistency.

I remember a game when I was Salford coach against Wigan, when we had a try disallowed that would have really set us rolling. We had got off to a flier and were 12–0 up, and the crowd was behind the team and me. We went in for a third try that would have put us 18–0 up, but the ref didn't even go to the big screen before ruling it out. My mood was hardly improved when Bill Arthur, Sky's touch-line reporter, collared me on the way to the dressing-room at half-time to tell me that the TV replays showed that it was a try. If the incident had been referred to the fourth official, it would definitely have been awarded. It's a good job Bill didn't have a microphone on me, or that would have been another hefty fine and a touch-line ban. We were really struggling for results at the time, and after that try had been disallowed, Wigan ran in three of their own in about seven minutes. Instead of being well on the way to pulling off a great victory, we were suddenly behind with the stuffing knocked out of us. For me, that simply highlighted the inconsistency of the officials, which I think is the biggest bugbear for everyone playing and coaching rugby league at any level. You watch any game, and you will see the sheer frustration on the players' faces at some time or another.

The best referees were, and remain, the ones you never saw during the game. When McCallum refereed, he was virtually anonymous for the 80 minutes – not through a lack of ability or control, but purely because he knew that he wasn't the man the fans had paid to see. I certainly couldn't imagine him ever having his own website or fan club, like Australia's Bill Harrigan does now. It was the same with Thompson, Lindop and the like. They just went out, got on with the job and had the confidence to make quick decisions. Invariably they were the correct ones as well – even if I wouldn't admit it at the time.

That's not to say that there hasn't been the odd memorable incident with referees in the current game. One of the funniest came when I went to watch Salford play St Helens recently. Something had gone on in the game, and Steve Blakeley, the Salford stand-off, said to ref Karl Kirkpatrick, 'Shouldn't you have given us a penalty for crossing for that?' Karl just ignored him, and nothing else was said. In the second half someone threw a pass to Steve, it ended up on the ground, and as Karl jogged past he said, 'Shouldn't you have caught that ball?' One–nil to the official on that occasion!

What also makes me laugh nowadays is when I hear people bagging Mike Stephenson, the Sky TV summariser, if video decisions go against their side. I'm sure that a lot of fans think that Stevo is the video ref. What they don't realise is that the fourth official sits in an entirely different place to the commentators, and makes his own mind up. I was at a game recently when a video decision went against the home side in the last minute, and Stevo got some terrible stick after the game. He was called a cheating so-and-so, amongst other things – but he was as much in the dark as everyone else about what the decision would be until it was made.

As both player and a coach I gave referees unbridled stick for 80 minutes, but it never carried on after the game. Everyone thinks I must hate Colin Morris, because he always seemed to send me off. But if I met him now we'd have a laugh and a drink, because I honestly don't have a problem with him. Or with any of the others, for that matter. During a match I would stoop to anything if I thought it would get us a decision, but away from the pitch there was none of that. There were times when I would question every single decision that was made, but I'm sure the refs will look back on it now and admit that they enjoyed it, just as I did. And one of the reasons for that, I'm certain, is that the standard of refereeing was higher during my playing career. But I do think that even then the refs would pick on players who had certain reputations. Kelvin Skerrett, for example, always seemed to get a raw deal.

Another thing that used to annoy me was that some of the refs did appear to be 'homers'. It was certainly true that the better the marks they used to get from the top clubs, the greater chance they had of being awarded the big games. I reckon there were some clubs that used to give the ref top marks because they knew that could help them with 50–50 decisions, especially at home. Not that it ever seemed to work for me when I was coaching at Salford.

I used to think it was a waste of time filling out the weekly post-match report about the referees. In fact, I never used to bother doing it – Graham McCarthy, the Salford secretary, filled them out for us. He always used to award them six or seven out of ten, whatever their performance. If he gave them a two or three, it wasn't worth the hassle of explaining it to the League.

When I was coming to the end at Salford, nothing seemed to go for us. If the ref went to the big screen, invariably the try would be awarded against us, or disallowed if we thought we had scored it. I'm sure that, over the course of a season, those decisions do tend to even themselves out – but when you are struggling, it seems that the world is against you. And the obvious person to blame for it all is, unfortunately, the referee.

People used to laugh at Salford because, at half-time or full time, I would be up and out of the dug-out straightaway. They all said that my pace and timing had gone, but that certainly wasn't the case, or I would never have managed to be one step behind the referee as he went down the tunnel, aiming a few well-chosen words of sarcasm in his direction. Neil Hilton and his guests in the top tier of the stand at the Willows used to kill themselves laughing, because they knew exactly what would happen each time the hooter went. But it was usually out of frustration because all I wanted was the two points, and at the time we weren't collecting many of them.

Lots of people used to think that we got preferential treatment from referees during my days at Wigan, but we honestly never used to discuss them. We knew that if we played as well as we could then we would pick up the points, however good or bad the official may be. Having said that, John Monie had a very clever way of registering his feelings with referees, without ever saying anything directly to them. If, for example, the referee hadn't awarded any penalties against the opposition for offside in the second half, John would position himself within earshot of the official in the players' bar after the match. He wouldn't speak directly to him, or have a go at his performance, but would say something like 'They are a superbly disciplined side, not to have conceded a penalty for offside in an entire half. That's something we will have to work on.' The ref would hear this, and the next time he was in charge at Central Park it would be at the back of his mind, and invariably we would get a couple of decisions in our favour.

I also remember at Wigan that Ellery and Shaun would be offside nine times out of ten, but it took about two years before anyone cottoned on to it. The opposition coaches would look at the video, see them coming back from an offside position and think, 'Hang about, they're coming back from an offside position.' All of a sudden we started getting a lot of penalties given against us for it – but it took a hell of a long time before people realised.

It wasn't only in England that referees seemed to have it in for Andy Gregory. When I had that spell with Illawarra we played a game against Newcastle Knights in Woollongong, and they absolutely murdered me. I had stitches in my mouth, around the outside of my mouth and above my eye. I remember Bob Millward, the big boss at Illawarra and father of St Helens coach Ian, citing two Newcastle players for punching me. When he told me that the players would be brought to book, it didn't take the pain away – but at least I felt that justice would be done. The next day the Australian disciplinary committee viewed the incidents, and I am sure they thought, 'It's only a little Pommie', because both Newcastle players escaped scot-free.

I'm not so certain they would have reached the same conclusion had I been the man in the dock. I am convinced that, over the years, things like that have coloured my judgement of officials – because it did seem that there was one rule for me and another for everyone else, whether it was in England or Australia. In fact, it almost reached the stage where I thought that if I was sitting on the toilet talking to myself, they would have hauled me in! No one would ever admit it, but I am sure they had it in for me.

TWENTY-THREE

Let Me Entertain You

Throughout my career I have been fortunate to play with some of the greatest names ever to grace a rugby field, and I would like to take this chance to pay my own little tribute to 13 of them. Over the next few pages I name the men I rate as the greatest entertainers I have shared a dressing-room with.

I know everyone has his or her own ideas about who should or shouldn't be in a Fantasy Rugby League XIII. The omission of Ellery and Shaun, for a start, will no doubt set tongues wagging that I have some sort of personal vendetta against them. But let me assure you, them, and everyone else that the team I list below is not one designed to get the best result in the world. I haven't selected the following 13 players to win any particular match, and I don't make any claims that they are the strongest, toughest or indeed most talented men I have played alongside.

The point of this is that I always thought of myself as an entertainer, someone who the crowd loved to watch on the field as much for the tricks I could pull off as for the result at the end of the 80 minutes. Likewise, the players I have chosen are those I rate as the best purely from an entertainment point of view. It isn't a side I feel would run the Aussies closest over the course of an Ashes series, or who would lift the World Cup – but it sure as hell would leave the crowd with a big smile on their face . . .

Full-back: MICK BURKE

People may tell you that size doesn't matter, but it certainly did for this guy, and what a reader of a game he was. And despite being such a big fellow, Mick certainly had plenty of pace – especially for someone so lazy! In fact, I would go so far as to say that Mick Burke is possibly the laziest trainer I ever had the pleasure to play with.

While myself and the rest of his Widnes team-mates – bar a certain man I will come to later – were running up and down Naughton Park, Mick would be standing at the other end of the field, practising his kicking. He would be there for ages, booting conversions or hoofing the ball downfield. The funny thing was, though, that he would never, ever retrieve his own balls. He used to send a young guy called Paul, who is now the kitman at Widnes, off to bring them back for him. Having said that, Mick had great ball skills and great vision, and was the rugby league version of Bobby Moore when it came to reading what was going to happen next.

Right wing: HENDERSON GILL

Gilly was an absolute cult hero on the Central Park terraces, and just edges out my old Widnes mucker Stuart Wright for the first winger's slot. I played countless games alongside him for Wigan and Great Britain, but at the end I was no nearer to understanding what he said than I was at the start. Not that that made any real difference to the pleasure I got from him.

Henderson played every game with total enthusiasm. Even if you were having a bad day, all you needed to do was look across at Gilly and you'd automatically have a smile on your face.

There is no doubt that the crowd absolutely adored him, and not just because of the wonderful tries he scored. There are too many of those to mention, although a couple do immediately spring to mind. The first was when he took on Hull's Gary Kemble in the 1985 Challenge Cup final to go over, and the second – of course – was one of his doubles for Great Britain against Australia in that memorable third Test win in Sydney in 1988. I haven't seen him for a while, but I hope his bloody dancing has improved since then!

Centre: JOE LYDON

If you were wondering who Mick Burke's partner was at Widnes when he used to get out of running and practise his kicking, then do so no longer. If Mick was the champion of laziness when it came to training, then Joe certainly ran him a very close second.

Having said that, there is no one I would sooner have in my side when it came to the big occasion. Time and again I would walk off the field shaking my head in disbelief at some of the things Joe managed to achieve on the biggest stages of all. It didn't matter whether it was a drop goal, an amazing burst of pace to go 60 yards and score, or whatever; he always seemed to pull something out of the hat when the eyes of the world were on us. Remember I told you about that incredible drop-goal from halfway in the 1989 Challenge Cup semi for Wigan against Warrington?

By his own admission, Joe was never a complete natural with the ball in his hands, but he had a great eye for a gap and was a fantastic kicker as well. He was second to none at creating space for others and the added bonus was that you knew you could always rely on him to make at least three tackles a game. Sometimes one after another, as well!

Centre: GENE MILES

Gene was coming towards the end of his career when he spent a season at Wigan, and that just makes you wonder how good it would have been to play alongside him when he was at his peak. He has to compare favourably with anyone who has ever played the game when it comes to skill and ball handling, and can certainly stand shoulder to shoulder with any of the many imports who have played in this country.

I played against him in Test matches at Lang Park and also in the Panasonic Cup final, when his Brisbane Broncos team beat Illawarra. He may have looked a serious character, but he had a great sense of humour – as well as one of the dodgiest of moustaches.

Everyone speaks of Andy Gregory, Shaun Edwards and Ellery Hanley as the three men who made Wigan tick, but during his season at Central Park Gene did more than anyone. Who could forget his performance when we put 70-odd points past Bradford in the Challenge Cup semi-final at Bolton? He ran the show from the off, and we were about 40–0 up at half-time. I still chuckle at the memory of following Bradford coach Peter Fox down the tunnel at the break and saying to Joe, 'We should be able to declare now.' Peter had a bit of a fiery temper to say the least, and I just managed to duck into the dressing-room before he whipped round to see who had said it. Blame Gene, Pete – he was the one who destroyed you.

Left wing: MARTIN OFFIAH

Martin is the quickest player I ever had the privilege to take the field with. He also suffered the most unjust criticism I have ever heard or read. No one who has ever played rugby league can be labelled a coward, yet there were plenty of people who gave Martin that tag. He also probably came in for more sledging than anyone else – and I hold my hands up and admit I was as guilty as anyone for it when he was at Widnes and I was at Wigan. In fact, you'd think the bloke had no legs judging from the number of times opposing players used to shout, 'Knock his f***ing head off!' Well, all I can say is that there were plenty who tried, but not so many who got within touching distance of him to carry it off. It says everything about the man's class that he has enjoyed such a prolific career without ever being seriously injured from someone connecting with him.

Martin used to pop up in the most ridiculous positions on the field – places he had no right to be. But he always seemed to end up in the right place – putting the ball down over the opponents' line. He was a true entertainer and absolutely brilliant to watch, even as a team-mate. He won games for Widnes, Wigan and Great Britain against the best and toughest opponents in the world. I suppose he will go down as another great Eddie MacDonald signing!

Stand-off: TONY MYLER

Tony is the closest thing you will ever see to a natural born rugby league superstar. I firmly believe that if he hadn't suffered such cruel fortune with injuries, he would have gone on to become Great Britain's most capped back. He had so much bad luck in that department that he even struggled to string together as many consecutive games as Joe did tackles!

I particularly remember him destroying Hull FC in the Premiership final at Headingley in 1983. He was 6ft 2in., but he had pace to go with his size and strength. But the one thing that really sticks out when you think of Tony Myler was his unbelievable ability with the ball in his hands. He was an absolute freak, with some of the things he used to do. Talent like that can't be coached into a man, you have to be born with it. Tony certainly was.

Scrum-half: PETER STERLING

I know he's an Aussie, and I know I never played alongside him – but I could hardly pick myself, could I? Peter had a great kicking game, great ball skills and great vision. His appetite for work was tremendous for a half-back, and he turned plenty of games with a single flash of brilliance. Maybe he wasn't an individual talent in the way that Alfie Langer is, but just ask anyone at Parramatta about him. It's just a pity, for Sterlo's sake, that he never really played well against me!

Prop: LEE CROOKS

Unfortunately, front-rowers like Crooksy are a dying breed in the modern game. God, I'm beginning to sound like one of those blokes who always harps on about the good old days now, aren't I?

Lee wasn't the toughest prop you would ever meet, but there were few I played with who had anything to compare with his ball handling skills and ability to offload in the tackle. He had a great kicking game, either from his hands or on the ground, with brilliant vision to boot. He was no slouch either, and was very light on his feet for a big fellow – apart from when he was leaving the Steyne Bar, near the Manly Pacific Hotel, during our days as Great Britain tourists.

Hooker: MARTIN DERMOTT

He was an absolute dream for any first receiver, because of that tremendous whipped, flat pass he had. We didn't need him to pick up the ball and scoot 30 yards at Wigan, because we had plenty of flair on the outside. That's why the first ball was so important, and Derms rarely failed to deliver in that department.

He was the complete footballer on the field, and an absolute nutter off it. I would also rate him as possibly the funniest player I have ever had the pleasure to line up with. In fact, I would like to express my belated gratitude to him here and now for one particular contribution he made when he was still at Central Park, but I had moved on to Leeds. I was suffering with a highly embarrassing problem at the time, but thanks to the dexterity of Martin Dermott's finger in one tackle – and he was quite deliberate in what he did – I have never had piles since. I only hope he washed his right hand after the game!

Prop: BRIAN LOCKWOOD

I definitely haven't picked him for his pace, that's one thing you can be sure of! I played with Brian at the start of my career at Widnes, and towards the end of his, but he was still a great man to have in your side. His skill level would have been unbelievable for a back, never mind a front-rower, and he was also a magnificent help to the kids in the side. I remember the year before I joined Widnes, when he sent Roger Millward over for a try as Hull KR won the Challenge Cup. The timing of that pass was worthy of winning the trophy alone.

Sadly, as with Lee Crooks, prop-forwards of the calibre of Brian Lockwood are dying out all too quickly.

Second row: MICK ADAMS

Mick was a brilliant organiser – he certainly organised my head early in my first Wembley final, when the huge crowd suddenly fazed me. Another great ball-handler, and a magnificent tactician to boot.

For a quiet fellow he was unbelievably tough. He just used to get on with his game, but opponents certainly knew when he had caught them. Mick wasn't blessed with a great deal of pace, but in that Widnes team, with him and Doug Laughton as playmakers, there was plenty to thrill the crowd. In fact, the only one who used to curse those two was Alan Dearden, who had to do all the tackling for them!

Second row: BOB ECCLES

Bob's selection might come as a bit of a surprise to some people, but I really rated this fellow. His record of tries for a back-row forward speaks for itself. He had bags of pace, and although he only came into the game late, he made up for lost time by fulfilling his ambition of playing for Great Britain.

Obviously, Bob needed someone to put him through the gap in the first place, but once he had the ball there was no stopping him. There are plenty of forwards these days who are looking for support after about five yards, but he always had the confidence in his own ability to make the line. And he usually did.

He was also a great companion to have around Warrington, particularly in 1986 when we were sitting in the boozer watching Australia stuff Great Britain after we'd both failed to make the side – although I still haven't forgiven him for telling me that Maurice Bamford had overlooked me again for the second Test!

Loose forward: STEVE NORTON

Knocker was the complete ball handler, and his vision was unbelievable. His array of tricks gave the Threepenny Stand at Hull plenty to marvel at, and it was a pleasure to be in the same Great Britain side as him. I am sure defences had no idea what he was going to do next.

I played with him in one particular Test match in France, and I must admit he had a funny way of warming up for an international. It comes in a bottle and it's red – but it didn't stop him having another superb game.

TWENTY-FOUR

To El and Back – The Pain in Spain

The idea of upping sticks and moving to Spain was first suggested to me when I attended the funeral of Mike Slater, a close friend of mine. Unknown to me it turned out to be the biggest load of bull I've ever heard. Some guy – it might as well have been Walter Mitty – told me about these great plans he had over there. In a nutshell, he promised me the earth and ended up costing me a fortune. He told me he had loads of property over there, and was building a bar and restaurant on an exclusive golf course. Like a mug, I took it all in. He had me in that much of a trance, he could have told me he was called Paul McKenna and I'd have believed him.

At the time he seemed believable enough. Remember, I had nothing lined up and nowhere to go after leaving the pub in Wigan, so I decided to take my chances and I moved out there with Alison. What a disaster that turned out to be. I went over for three days by myself at first to check it all out. He was living out there, and I have to admit that it was a lovely place. I met him again, we had a more detailed chat and he told me all his plans. He showed me this place, which he claimed to own, and said that Ali and me could live there. How was I to know it was all a load of rubbish?

The first alarm bells started ringing when we arrived, and there was no apartment sorted for us. It also transpired that the supposed bar on the golf course was a figment of his imagination. And no one he introduced me to ever seemed to have a Christian name – he told me he had a million friends, but I never saw any of them. We moved into his place with him for a while, but eventually we had to find somewhere to live, and ended up getting a place in San Pedro, near Marbella. I also had to find a job and eventually landed one with Global FM, an English-speaking radio station for ex-pats about 30 minutes away.

I was having something to eat one day in San Pedro when someone recognised me, and we just got chatting about sport. One of the lads I got talking to worked for Global, and I asked him if they had a sports programme. He said not, so I suggested presenting one for them. A couple of days later he got back to me and said they were up for it, so I moved into the radio business. It was no small-time thing either – it went out live between three and seven, and covered a vast area from Nerja to Gibraltar, all the way down the Costa Del Sol. It made a change to be doing the interviewing, and I had some big names on – people such as Steve McManaman, Ian Rush, Neil Fairbrother, Alex Murphy and Shaun Edwards. And I had a great chat with Ken Jones of the *Independent*, a good mate and a superb journalist, who has covered everything from World Cups to Muhammad Ali's heavyweight fights.

The big problem was that the show never had a major sponsor, despite Global's insistence that they were going to get one lined up. When I had started, they had told me they would need some sponsorship to sort out my wages. After about four weeks, when I still hadn't received any money, I started to get a bit twitchy. After about six weeks, I went in as usual to do my show and arrived at 2.45 p.m., all ready to roll. I asked where my money was, and they told me I'd be paid the following Tuesday. I said, 'That's fine, I'll do my show on Tuesday then.' I turned round and walked out, and that was that.

By this stage I had already been featured in the rugby league press back home – it seemed that if Andy Gregory wasn't doing anything story-wise, they would make something up. The tale this time was that I had done a runner from England, among other things. I can't say too much about it because, although I had ignored a lot of similar crap about me in the past, this cut a bit deeper – so I put it all in the hands of my solicitor. That particular tale will come out in time, but here and now is not the place.

Suffice to say that it really did annoy me, because I kept myself to myself in Spain and was only interested in getting my life back on an even keel. I had worked hard to cope with my depression, and the drinking had dropped off dramatically. If you can stay off the beer completely in Spain then you are a one-off, and I never said that I would turn my back on drinking entirely. But I had cut my intake in half, and that was very much a step in the right direction. I remember Ali turning to me one day and saying, 'You're doing really well,' and that one sentence meant so much. It is very easy to slag people off, but when you are trying your hardest and you get a pat on the back from someone close to you, it is a great feeling and makes you even more determined to succeed.

Evidently that still wasn't enough to stop all the rumours.

Since I've been back in England I have heard a tale that I only left Spain because I had a fight in a pub and left two people for dead, and the Spanish police were after me. Another story linked me with the tobacco and drinks black market. But the worst was that I'd only come back to set up a deal to import drugs, and as soon as everything was in place I would be heading back to Spain. For someone whose next cigarette will be his first, that was unbelievable.

After I quit the radio station there was not a lot to stay out there for. I had no work, no money coming in, and I couldn't see how we were going to make ends meet. So I bought a second-hand car, and we decided to head back to England. Talk about the incredible journey! I had hardly any money in my pocket, but we managed to limp our way through France, Ali, my two dogs and myself all sleeping in the car. We had run into problems while we were still in Spain, because someone stole my driving licence and other documents, so I had to get a letter from the police explaining the situation just in case we got stopped on the way over.

On the day when we finally arrived within sight of the English Channel, we were virtually out of both money and petrol. We had managed to buy some food for the dogs, while Ali and I shared a packet of digestive biscuits between us. We'd have one each every half-hour or so, and she made me laugh when she looked at me and said, 'They don't half take the edge off your appetite, don't they?'

We'd been driving for 1,700 miles when we saw a sign that told us that we were 30 km from St Malo. We were so low on fuel that we actually ran out as we drove into the petrol station. We had about £20 in pesetas between us, and no French money, but the guy only took credit cards – he wouldn't entertain the idea of us giving him Spanish cash. Fortunately, a Frenchman pulled up who spoke good English. I explained the situation to him, and I managed to persuade him to put £10 worth of petrol in the car in return for our twenty quid's worth of pesetas. That would be enough to get us to St Malo, and from there I wasn't bothered. Even if we had to push the car on, and do the same to get off at the other end, that was fair enough. I just wanted to be docking in Portsmouth.

We didn't have a penny in our pockets, we were both feeling shattered and very low after a 1,700-mile trip, but at least we could look forward to sailing home the next morning. The ferry was booked and the tickets had been paid for – John Marsden, a good mate of mine from back home, had stayed with us for a week and lent us the money to sort that out – so that looked like an end to our problems. Some chance! We still had the two dogs with us, Hatti the Dalmatian and a Japanese Akita called Bailey, because we had paid the necessary money to bring them out of Spain. They'd had their inoculations and everything, so we didn't think there would be any problem. But the next morning, when we got to the terminal to get on to the ferry, we were told that the dogs hadn't got the necessary jabs to come back to England. It was my own fault – but there was no way they would let them come with us. I had no money to pay for their injections, so they would have to stay in St Malo.

Ali and I discussed whether we should explain the situation to the British Embassy, because I had no joy trying to get some money wired over from England. And to make matters worse, it was a Bank Holiday weekend, which didn't help. Eventually we went to the tourist board office in St Malo and a girl lent me £50, but as security I had to leave her our tickets for the ferry, which had been rescheduled for three days later, as well as my passport. That was enough to get the dogs injected, but it only left us with a tenner until we sailed.

As we were leaving the tourist board office we bumped into a gang of Brits, and one of them shouted me over. It turned out to be a guy called Tony Bolland, who was born near to where I was in Hindley, but had since moved to Jersey. Twelve of his mates had been out there for a few days and had an absolute scream. We told them all about our trip, and Tony booked us into a hotel and lent me a few bob to see us through. His generosity was out of this world and really bailed us out of trouble. We owe him a massive favour, and I only hope that one day I am in a position to repay him.

We managed to get on the ferry without any further problems, but when we arrived in England we were told that, unfortunately, I hadn't been out of the country for six months, and so we had to leave the dogs in quarantine. Again that was my fault, because I hadn't checked the rules and regulations – but the whole thing had become a joke. If I was going back to Spain with the dogs, I could drive them all the way through France with no questions asked. As an exercise in bureaucracy, it's just a massive money-spinner.

When we arrived in Portsmouth I filled the car up, we got something to eat, and we managed to reach the Daresbury Park Hotel by 11.15 p.m. Richard Gray, the general manager, was absolutely superb to us. He didn't know we were coming, but he found us a room straightaway, and I can't thank him enough. Unfortunately, after ten days, the hotel was completely booked up, so I was off hunting for a place to stay again. I spoke to my pal Roy Jackson from Express Electricals, who I'd done a lot of work with during my days with Wigan. He used to provide me with a beautiful white Mercedes as a sponsored car, and I'd like to think that we were good for each other.

As I was driving over to meet Roy, he rang me on the mobile phone I had borrowed to tell me about a wine bar in King's

Street in Wigan. At the time I had no intention of going back into that business, but I met him and another couple of guys, Chris and Danny Baybutt, who wanted me to run the place for them. So I told them how I saw it going: I wanted to call it Gregory's Sports Bar, and I would just pop in now and again. I certainly didn't plan on spending all my life behind a bar, and so I spoke to Steve Peters, the old St Helens scrum-half who works for the Wigan Beer Company, to see if he could help me find someone to run it. He put me in touch with a guy who had apparently just left Ashton Golf Club, who duly arrived and Roy gave him the float for the tills.

Throughout my brief involvement with the place, I never actually went behind the bar to pull a pint or touched a till. After the first few days Roy, Chris and David told me that the money in the till didn't add up correctly. They decided to carry on, but when they had a stock check three days later, it didn't tally again. The lad behind the bar left immediately, and when I saw Roy again it was mentioned about me going in full time. No way was I going to get involved to that extent. I had already put myself under an enormous amount of pressure to get the thing up and running again; for example, I had been trying to get the televisions installed in time for Euro 2000, but a seemingly little job like getting the TV aerials fixed up turned into a day-long headache because we couldn't get anyone to fit them in a three-storey building. I knew that turning my back on it would put me in difficult circumstances, because once again I would have no money coming in. But at least I knew I would be healthy, even if not as wealthy as I could have been.

Since I arrived back from Spain I haven't been all that bothered about going into pubs, let alone having one of my own again. While all my old hunger for rugby league has returned, if I'd returned to the pub game I would have been back to square one. I have started doing some more radio work, I'm hoping to get some after-dinner speaking engagements, and I don't think this sport will ever leave me now. It is always going to be a part of my life in some capacity.

When I was in Spain I kept in regular contact with Cliff Fleming, from Wigan St Pat's. I had known for years that the club needed some attention, because it just wasn't the same. The standards had dropped off a lot over the seasons. In fact, while I was in San Pedro, I bumped into a couple of blokes from an amateur club in Yorkshire, who told me that my old side had gone right down the pan. I know that they will probably never enjoy such a golden era as they had in the past, when players such as Mike Gregory, Joe Lydon, Andy Platt and myself all came through together. All the kids are snapped up straightaway by professional clubs these days, so it would be virtually impossible to repeat. But even accounting for that, the club had slipped dramatically.

Dave Ruddy and Jimmy Taylor were still coaching St Pat's when I returned from Spain, but I knew that a job would be available in some form. So I sent a letter to the committee, who asked Dave and Jimmy if they were in favour of my coming on board with them, and they both agreed. Those two have worked their fingers to the bone for St Pat's, but they accepted that some sort of change was needed, and I can assure everyone that I am 100 per cent committed to them. Obviously, if a job with a professional club comes along, then I would have to consider it, but for now I am more than happy putting something back into the club which helped me so much as a youngster.

The players have responded superbly as well. At their first pre-season training session a year ago only four turned up. This time we had 38 – and that was in Wigan Week as well. Years ago, all the factories in town used to shut down for the first two weeks in July, and the whole place just stopped. It isn't quite the same any more, but it still grinds to a halt to a large extent – so to get that number to my first session was a feat in itself.

Because it was the first one, I don't think the lads would have let me get away without joining in – and so I did. And it didn't take long for them to start giving me stick, either, when I made a couple of mistakes in a game of tick-and-pass. I could have lived with that – but it was when I fell over and cut my knee and smashed my finger that it really hit home that maybe I wasn't as young as I thought! But, all in all, I felt great afterwards, if a little stiff.

The old buzz is back, and I really can't wait to get going again. I don't think I will reach the stage where I dust the old boots down and get out there among them for an actual game, but I am loving everything about it. Andy Gregory is ready to go once again – and this time there will be no mistakes.